Sociological
Approaches
to the
Old
Testament

Sociological Approaches to the Old Testament

by
Robert R. Wilson

Fortress Press
Philadelphia

Library of Congress Cataloging in Publication Data

Wilson, Robert R., 1942–
    Sociological approaches to the Old Testament.

    (Guides to Biblical scholarship)
    1. Sociology, Biblical. 2. Bible. O.T.—Criticism,
interpretation, etc. 3. Jews—Politics and government
—To 70 A.D. I. Title. II. Series.
BS1199.S6W54   1984   220.6'01   83–16607
ISBN 0–8006–0469–5

K487H83   Printed in the United States of America   1–469

For Sharyn

Editor's Foreword

In recent years biblical scholars have come to focus more and more attention on the application of data, methods and theories from the social sciences to the study of the Bible. Many have come to recognize the value of information and perspectives from modern sociology and anthropology in particular, and the importance of questions concerning social roles and structures. A great many specialized studies have addressed specific problems raised by the Old Testament and the history of ancient Israel, and broad interpretations of the Old Testament from such perspectives have begun to appear. Moreover, several working groups and seminars in the Society of Biblical Literature are exploring the potential usefulness of sociological perspectives.

But, as Professor Wilson demonstrates in this volume, the application of sociological methods to biblical study is by no means new. On the contrary, it is as old as the disciplines of sociology and anthropology. And the basic questions—if not the critical methods—of sociology were important even to authors of biblical books. The difference in the present day is the availability of a wider range of sociological and anthropological data and approaches, generating fresh theories with the potential to open new perspectives on the biblical material.

In the present volume Professor Wilson surveys and evaluates the history of the sociological study of the Old Testament, identifies major approaches in use today, and sets out some guidelines for the application of the methods and data to the investigation of the Old Testament. He demonstrates with test cases some of the ways sociology—in concert with other methods—has been and can be useful to the student of the Old Testament.

Broadly speaking, sociological approaches are valuable in two related but distinct disciplines of biblical study, exegesis and history. For the historian of ancient Israel sociology provides not evidence for events, but tools for analyzing the ancient evidence, and theories about the way society developed. Ethnographic evidence from contemporary tribal societies provides analogies to circumstances in ancient Israel which are likely to be closer than those derived from modern industrial society. With regard to exegesis, sociology provides ways of relating the origin, transmission, and meaning of texts to social roles, groups, and structures. It stresses to the interpreter of the Old Testament what was fundamental to ancient Israel, the importance of the group, the society, the people.

Emory University　　　　　　　　　　　　　　　　GENE M. TUCKER
Atlanta, Georgia
Summer, 1983

Contents

CONTENTS

Abbreviations

AA	*American Anthropologist*
BA	*Biblical Archaeologist*
BASOR	*Bulletin of the American Schools of Oriental Research*
CBQ	*Catholic Biblical Quarterly*
HUCA	*Hebrew Union College Annual*
IEJ	*Israel Exploration Journal*
Int	*Interpretation*
JBL	*Journal of Biblical Literature*
JRAI	*Journal of the Royal Anthropological Institute*
JSOT	*Journal for the Study of the Old Testament*
SBLSP	*Society of Biblical Literature, Seminar Papers*
SJA	*Southwestern Journal of Anthropology*
TZ	*Theologische Zeitschrift*
VT	*Vetus Testamentum*
VTSup	Vetus Testamentum, Supplements
ZAW	*Zeitschrift für die alttestamentliche Wissenschaft*

I

Old Testament Scholarship and the Study of Society

The word "sociology" can have two meanings. In a narrow sense, the word refers to that branch of the social sciences which is concerned with those patterns of social conduct that are produced by human social interaction and value orientation. In a more general sense, "sociology" may simply refer to the study of society. When used in this way, the term may embrace any of the social sciences (sociology, economics, anthropology, political science, and psychology), or it may refer loosely to the analysis of any aspect of social life.[1] Sociology narrowly defined is a fairly late arrival on the academic scene and was not recognized as an independent discipline until the nineteenth century. However, scholarly interest in general sociological issues is much older and is deeply rooted in the western intellectual tradition. It is therefore not surprising that biblical scholars have always made use of sociological data, both in the interpretation of the Old Testament text and in the reconstruction of ancient Israelite history.

SOCIOLOGY AND THE OLD TESTAMENT INTERPRETER

Long before the social sciences emerged as distinct scholarly disciplines, medieval commentators occasionally sought to explain an enigmatic passage by setting it in a specific social context. They also inquired about the social background of unusual customs mentioned in the text and sometimes dabbled in psychology by supplying a motive for a character's otherwise inexplicable actions. To be sure, many of these early sociological comments strike the modern reader as fanciful. Often they are not based on solid evidence but on untested generalizations drawn from common life experiences. It is difficult to take seriously the rabbinic attempt to determine the

---

1. Bert F. Hoselitz, ed., *A Reader's Guide to the Social Sciences*, rev. ed. (New York: Free Press, 1970), p. 1.

1

compositional order of the three biblical books attributed to Solomon by supposing that he wrote Song of Songs in the passion of his youth, Proverbs in the wisdom of his middle years, and Ecclesiastes in the cynicism of his old age.[2] Similarly, the attempt of various commentators to describe the psychological traits that led Moses to murder the Egyptian (Exod. 2:11–25) clearly imports alien concepts into the biblical text.[3] Still the resort to a sociological approach does indicate that some early interpreters recognized the importance of reading biblical texts in the light of specific social contexts.

Interest in sociological issues is noticeable particularly in the work of scholars who were concerned to ground all interpretation in a literal reading of the text. Thus, for example, Hugh of St. Victor (d. 1141) insisted that commentators should not move to an allegorical or spiritual interpretation of a passage before expounding it literally. Such a literal reading initially requires an examination of the text's grammar and syntax and may also include uncovering the peculiar idiom of the biblical writer in order to determine the "sense" of the text. Hugh illustrates this point by referring to an obscure prophecy: "And seven women shall take hold of one man in that day, saying, 'We will eat our own bread and wear our own clothes, only let us be called by your name; take away our reproach'" (Isa. 4:1). According to Hugh, the sense of this text is to be found by seeing it against the historical background of war and the resulting destruction of the male population. An understanding of the women's comments can be achieved only by knowing something about Israelite culture and by recognizing the social stigma which ancient Israel attached to women unable to marry and bear children.[4] A similar concern with the literal sense of the text can be seen in the work of the great Jewish interpreter Rashi (1040–1105). In this case too, a stress on the literal meaning occasionally led to the use of sociological observations as part of the interpretive process. Some of Rashi's disciples, including Samuel ben Meir (Rashbam) and Joseph Bekhor Shor, even went so far as to draw on their own knowledge of contemporary social customs in order to expound a verse.[5]

2. "R. Jonathan said: 'He [Solomon] first wrote The Song of Songs, then Proverbs, then Ecclesiastes.' R. Jonathan argues from the way of the world. When a man is young he composes songs; when he grows older he makes sententious remarks; when he becomes an old man he speaks of the vanity of things" (*Cant. Rab.* 1:1, 10). Maurice Simon, trans., "Song of Songs," in *Midrash Rabbah*, ed. H. Freedman and Maurice Simon (London: Soncino Press, 1939), 9:17.

3. For examples of such psychological interpretations, see Brevard S. Childs, *The Book of Exodus: A Critical Theological Commentary* (Philadelphia: Westminster Press, 1974), pp. 40–42.

4. For a discussion of this example and Hugh's general views on interpretation, see Beryl Smalley, *The Study of the Bible in the Middle Ages* (Notre Dame, Ind.: University of Notre Dame Press, 1964), pp. 83–106.

5. Smalley, *Study of the Bible*, pp. 149–53.

Although medieval commentators only occasionally showed any interest in sociological matters, subsequent interpreters gradually came to recognize the importance of understanding the Old Testament's social context. The coming of the Renaissance brought a rebirth of interest in textual studies and in the history of Israel and its neighboring civilizations. At first through the reading of classical texts and eventually through actual exploration and excavation, scholars began to study the societies of the ancient Near East. Although commentators used this extra-biblical material in different ways, there was a growing tendency to believe that comparative data could aid in interpreting the Old Testament. This tendency continued until the latter part of the nineteenth century, when the comparative approach became an important component of the historical-critical method.[6]

Even though seventeenth and eighteenth century interpreters made increasing use of comparative evidence, they were not always clear about their reasons for doing so. However, it is likely that they felt more keenly the same problem already recognized by Hugh of St. Victor. They realized that a sizable historical gap separated them from the biblical period, and they suspected that the Old Testament contained historical and cultural allusions that obscured the meaning of the text. These allusions might be clarified by applying a comparative approach that would supply more knowledge of ancient Near Eastern societies in general and ancient Israelite society in particular. This point of view was strongly supported by the historical-critical scholars of the nineteenth century, who stressed the time-bound character of the biblical writings. These scholars also focused their attention on the methodological difficulties involved in interpreting ancient documents. This methodological self-consciousness touched off hermeneutical debates that continue to the present day.

The Problem of Reading Ancient Texts

Any given text may be interpreted from a variety of different perspectives, depending on the interests and goals of the interpreter. However, all acceptable interpretations, no matter how divergent, must have one thing in common. They must all be based on a valid understanding of the text which they are interpreting. At the root of

---

6. For a general history of interpretation in this period, see S. L. Greenslade, ed., *The Cambridge History of the Bible: The West from the Reformation to the Present Day* (Cambridge: At the University Press, 1963).

the problem of interpretation, then, is the question of how texts are to be read and understood.

It is not necessary here to discuss all of the difficulties encountered by readers of ancient texts, but a general sketch of the process of reading will help to clarify the role that sociology plays in Old Testament interpretation. In every act of reading, there is a communications gap between the reader and the text. This gap is present even if the text's author is a contemporary of the reader, but it becomes progressively larger as the temporal, cultural, and spacial distance between reader and author increases. On one side of the communications gap is the text itself. The text is the creation of an author, who shapes it to reflect a view of reality that is intended to have an impact of some sort on the reader. The author may wish to convey information or opinions to the reader or may simply wish to evoke an emotional response. In any case, the vehicle of this attempt at communication is the text, which is created by using the language, literary forms, and symbols commonly understood in the author's society. The influence of society is thus present at two levels in the creation of the text. At the first level, the author's worldview is an amalgamation of personal insights and the views of the surrounding society. At the second level, the literary expression of the worldview is the result of the author's creative use of the society's language and literary conventions.

On the other side of the communications gap is the reader. Like the author, the reader brings to the text a personal view of the world and specific linguistic and literary conventions that are socially conditioned. Even if the reader and the author live in the same society at the same time, their perceptions of reality and patterns of linguistic usage will not be congruent because of the idiosyncratic factors involved. The reader must attempt to overcome this lack of congruence in order to understand the author's text. In the act of reading, two goals must be accomplished. First, it is necessary for the reader to become conscious of personal predispositions and understandings so as not to impose them on the text. Second, it is necessary for the reader to become informed about the author's understandings and literary conventions. At an elementary level, this means that the reader must know the basic language of the text, along with any related idioms or special dialects. At a more sophisticated level, the reader must seek to understand the text's literary devices and allusions and the worldview that they express.[7]

7. For a more thorough discussion of the reading process, see Wolfgang Iser, *The Act of Reading* (Baltimore: Johns Hopkins University Press, 1978), pp. 31–35; and Stanley Fish, *Is There a Text in This Class?* (Cambridge, Mass.: Harvard University Press, 1980), pp. 21–67.

Because of the subjectivity involved both on the part of the reader and on the part of the author, a definitive understanding of a text can never be achieved. Different readers will see slightly different things in the same text. However, each of these divergent readings can be considered valid so long as it is an *informed* reading that is aware of the conventions being employed by both reader and author. The hallmark of a valid reading is that it can be recognized as valid by other informed readers of the same text. These two safeguards—the text itself and the community of informed readers—prevent individual interpretations from becoming overly subjective.

When the process of reading is understood, it is easy to see why ancient texts are so difficult to interpret. Given the age of the texts, the very things that the reader needs to know in order to become an *informed* reader are difficult to discover. The basic language of the text may be imperfectly understood, and crucial technical terms may be altogether obscure. The literary genres employed may be unfamiliar to the modern reader, and the worldview of the text may be a foreign one. For this reason readers of ancient texts have often employed data drawn from outside of the texts themselves in order to aid the process of interpretation. In the case of the Old Testament, interpreters have used comparative philology and ancient Near Eastern texts to throw more light on the culture and thought patterns of the biblical writers. In the same way, insights from the social sciences can help the interpreter to understand the sociology of ancient Israel and the sociological dimensions òf the interpretive process itself. The research tools developed by the social sciences are specifically designed to deal with the sorts of sociological questions which the interpreter must answer in order to become an informed reader. As an adjunct to other types of comparative approaches, a sociological approach can provide useful information at several points in the reading process.

The Role of Sociology in
Old Testament Interpretation

The Sociology of the Interpreter

As we have already noted, one of the first tasks of the interpreter is to become aware of personal assumptions and understandings that might influence the interpretation of a text or make the reading process more difficult. Many of these assumptions and understandings have a sociological component, and the social sciences can help the reader to be self-conscious about the role that social and cultural forces play in shaping literary perceptions. Each of us approaches the Old Testament with a view of reality that has been nurtured by the social and cultural situations in which we have lived. We possess well-developed notions about the way the world operates and the way a healthy society functions. We hold certain ethical values and religious positions. Because of our cultural backgrounds and educational experiences, we have varying degrees of linguistic competence and literary sensitivity. By becoming aware of all of these factors, we can avoid identifying our own perceptions with those of the biblical text. We can also see more clearly the differences between our world and the world of the Old Testament writers. Being aware of these differences may help us to focus on those features of the Old Testament worldview about which we need more information in order to become informed readers.

The Sociology of the Old Testament

Just as the worldview of the reader is socially shaped, so also the perceptions and literary conventions of the Old Testament writers bear the stamp of their social and cultural situation. The social sciences can sometimes contribute to our understanding of the authors' world by providing useful analogies from studies of modern societies. These contributions can come at several levels. At the linguistic level, studies of oral tradition and the function of literary genres may provide a more detailed knowledge of similar phenomena in the biblical period. For the most part, we do not live in a society where oral traditions flourish, and our experience with written literature is usually limited to a few well-defined genres. Yet biblical scholars agree that much of the Old Testament is the crystallization of complex oral traditions. These traditions were transmitted from one generation to the next by clothing them in various literary forms, some of which are not commonly found in our society. The oral genres were eventually frozen in writing and are preserved in our present biblical text. A more comprehensive understanding of this written literature can be achieved by becoming aware of the way in which the original oral genres functioned in their social settings and were finally transmitted to the biblical writers. Even though we may not be familiar with certain literary genres, anthropologists and folklorists have studied some of them extensively in modern societies where oral literature is still created and preserved. This contemporary evidence can shed new light on the characteristics of oral literature and help us to become better informed about the Old Testament's literary conventions.

6

At the cultural level, social scientific studies of the way modern societies function may shed some light on the social structures and cultural institutions of ancient Israel. The worldview of the biblical writers was shaped by a society very different from the modern industrialized societies with which we are familiar. The Old Testament is filled with references to various aspects of this society and to the cultural phenomena which it contained. Some of these references may be unintelligible to us if we have no additional information from ancient sources or from archaeological excavations and if we know of no comparable phenomena in our own society. In such cases we may be able to supplement our regular sources of information by drawing on social scientific research conducted in modern societies having a social structure similar to that of ancient Israel. To be sure, each society is in a sense unique, and it would be misleading to assume that ancient Israelite society can be reconstructed solely on the basis of modern analogues. Still, if the sociological information is used judiciously so that the unique features of Israelite society are not obscured, a social scientific approach can bring us closer to the world of the biblical writers than would be possible if we relied on our own cultural experiences.

Finally, at the theological level, the social sciences can sometimes provide a more profound understanding of Israel's faith. Such an understanding is absolutely essential if we are to appropriate the Old Testament theologically, for theological reflection must begin with an accurate knowledge of Israelite religious beliefs. The social sciences help us to acquire this knowledge in the first instance by playing their normal role in the overall exegetical process, and in this sense they help to lay the interpretive foundation for our theological use of the text. In addition, the social sciences can sometimes shed light on specific religious phenomena which were common in ancient Israel but are poorly attested in our own society. These phenomena are often the primary focus of Old Testament literature, and a thorough understanding of them is crucial to an informed reading of the Bible. Yet basic components of Israelite religion, such as prophecy and sacrifice, are not usually part of our own religious experience and cannot be understood adequately on the basis of textual or archaeological evidence alone. A more sophisticated appreciation of these unfamiliar phenomena can come from the data gathered by social scientists investigating societies having religious practices similar to those of ancient Israel. As is also the case with other aspects of culture, it is important to recognize the uniqueness of religious events and experiences. Yet sociological research suggests that religious phenomena in a number of different societies may exhibit common structural patterns and social functions. When this sort of comparative evidence is used with caution, it can enlarge our understanding of Israel's religion and draw us more deeply into the religious perceptions of the biblical writers.

SOCIOLOGY AND THE HISTORIAN

Just as sociology plays an important role in the process of Old Testament interpretation, so also the social sciences can provide useful tools for students of ancient Israelite history. Sociological approaches can aid historians in a number of different ways but are particularly helpful in the task of defining an area of study and interpreting historical sources.

The Historian as Sociologist

One of the major contributions of the social sciences has been to underscore the complexity of social organizations. All societies, whether modern or ancient, advanced or "primitive," are complicated webs of interpersonal and intergroup relationships. Historians hoping to reconstruct ancient societies must take this complexity into account in their work. It is no longer sufficient for the historian to write the history of a society by concentrating on only one of its components. Rather, the historian must attempt to deal with all of the elements of the society and their interaction over a specified period of time. The social sciences thus help the historian to delineate new areas that must be investigated and to formulate new questions to ask of the ancient sources.

This contribution of the social sciences is particularly significant for historians of ancient Israel, who in the past have tended to concentrate on Israel's political and religious history.[8] In interpreting the available archaeological and textual data, they have inquired primarily about the light that their evidence might throw on governmental institutions or on the nature of the cult. The social sciences suggest additional questions that might also be fruitfully asked. Up to this point there have been few systematic attempts to sift the archaeological data for evidence on how ancient Israelites went about their daily lives and ran their economy. Their administrative and judicial systems require more definition, and even the nature of their religious system outside of Jerusalem is unclear. More needs to

---

8. On this point see Norman K. Gottwald, "Sociological Method in the Study of Ancient Israel," in *Encounter with the Text*, ed. Martin J. Buss (Philadelphia: Fortress Press, 1979), pp. 69–81.

be known about the social structure and the composition of the population. The interaction of all of the elements of the social system has yet to be studied in detail, and it remains to be determined whether or not the social system was consistent throughout the whole land. To be sure, it may not be possible for the historian to achieve significant results in some of these areas because of a lack of evidence. However, the asking of new questions may lead to unexpected discoveries and may yield a more detailed historical picture which will benefit both the historian and the Old Testament interpreter.

The Historian and the Sources

In addition to helping the historian define new areas of inquiry, the social sciences aid in the interpretation of ancient sources. Every Israelite historian must be an interpreter of the Old Testament, for the Old Testament remains our major source of information about biblical Israel. The historian must also make use of texts from the ancient Near East and must correlate the textual evidence with the available archaeological data. We have already noted the difficulties involved in reading ancient texts and the way in which a sociological approach lessens these difficulties. The historian can thus benefit from the contribution of the social sciences in the same way that any Old Testament interpreter does. Furthermore, the historian can use information supplied by cross-cultural studies to fill in gaps in the ancient evidence and reconstruct a more complete picture of Israelite society.[9]

However, just as the general reader of the Old Testament must be cautious when using sociological approaches as part of the interpretive process, so also the historian must be aware of the methodological difficulties involved in using modern sociological evidence to reconstruct ancient societies. The danger of forcing biblical Israel into a modern sociological mold is ever present and must be avoided at all costs. It is therefore necessary for anyone using sociological methods to understand their strengths and weaknesses and to formulate guidelines to govern the use of such methods in Old Testament criticism.

9. For a discussion of the goals and methods of the Old Testament historian, see J. Maxwell Miller, *The Old Testament and the Historian* (Philadelphia: Fortress Press, 1976), pp. 1–19; and George W. Ramsey, *The Quest for the Historical Israel* (Atlanta: John Knox Press, 1981), pp. 3–23.

9

II

Sociology in
Old Testament Criticism:
History and Method

THE RISE OF THE SOCIAL SCIENCES

The study of society is by no means a new phenomenon. In the Old Testament itself, the Deuteronomists set out a general outline of the ideal Israelite state (Deuteronomy 12—26). Somewhat later, both Plato and Aristotle wrote treatises on political and social organization. During the Middle Ages, Renaissance, and Reformation, theories about society continued to be advanced, usually by theologians and philosophers. The pattern of sociological research established in this early period continued until the eighteenth century. Sociology normally took the form of social theory and was clearly tangential to other academic interests. Although important sociological contributions were made by a few individuals, such as Hobbes and Locke, most scholars preferred to concentrate on philosophy, law, history, and the rapidly emerging natural sciences. This pattern began to change in the eighteenth century, when scholars again became interested in the study of society, and renewed scholarly interest finally led in the nineteenth century to the emergence of the social sciences (sociology, anthropology, economics, political science, and psychology) as distinct academic disciplines.

There is no simple explanation for the rise of the social sciences, but certainly several major factors were involved. First, the eighteenth century was a period of social change throughout much of Europe. The middle class emerged as a major force in political and economic life, and the industrial revolution brought about sweeping changes in working conditions and living patterns. These developments focused popular attention on social and economic problems and prompted scholars to analyze the traumatic events that were taking place. The center of scholarly interest thus shifted from social theory to the study of living societies.

Second, during the eighteenth and nineteenth centuries humanistic scholarship was gradually freed from the constricting influences of theology and philosophy. Although later research would provide a painful reminder that no scholarship is without presuppositions and intellectual influences, early humanists relished the freedom to define their own areas of research and to develop new methodologies. Turning away from traditional historical, theological, and philosophical issues, they found new fields for research in the natural and social sciences.

Third, the growth of the natural sciences undoubtedly stimulated the development of approaches to the study of society. The scientific method, which formulated hypotheses and then submitted them to unbiased testing through controlled experiments, exerted a powerful influence on scholars in other disciplines. Early social scientists believed that the methods of the natural sciences could be transferred to sociological research and could provide the objectivity necessary for their discipline's academic respectability.

Finally, the rise of the social sciences can be attributed in part to the general intellectual ferment and interdisciplinary interests of the nineteenth century. Scientific discoveries were occurring at a rapid rate, and systematic exploration led to the accumulation of massive amounts of new data on ancient and modern societies. At the same time, various academic disciplines were formulating comprehensive theories to account for new data, and when these theories were successful, other disciplines often borrowed them and applied them to new areas of inquiry. The clearest example of this sort of influence can be seen in the natural sciences, where Darwin's theory of evolution had a profound influence on other academic disciplines, including the social sciences.[1]

Once the social sciences emerged as distinct disciplines, they quickly began to influence other disciplines, including biblical studies. Although Old Testament scholars have traditionally been interested in most of the issues dealt with by social scientists, only two of the social sciences—sociology and anthropology—have persistently exerted an influence on biblical studies, while one, psychology, has had a peripheral impact. Before looking at the way that Old Testament critics have used social scientific approaches, it will be

---

1. For a brief history of social scientific research before the nineteenth century, see Bert F. Hoselitz, "The Social Sciences in the Last Two Hundred Years," in *A Reader's Guide to the Social Sciences*, ed. Bert F. Hoselitz, 1st ed. (New York: Free Press, 1959), pp. 7-25; and Margaret T. Hodgen, *Early Anthropology in the Sixteenth and Seventeenth Centuries* (Philadelphia: University of Pennsylvania Press, 1964).

helpful to consider these particular social sciences in greater detail in order to clarify their distinctive interests and methods.

Sociology

Sociology is the branch of the social sciences that is concerned with ". . . the regularities in social conduct that are due neither to psychological traits of individuals nor to their rational economic decisions but that are produced by the social conditions in which they find themselves."[2] These social conditions include not only the complex relationships that normally exist between individuals in a society but also the beliefs and values that people hold about themselves and others. Sociologists are thus interested both in human interaction and in personal attitudes about individuals and groups within the social structure.

The most characteristic feature of sociology, and the one which helps to distinguish it from its nearest neighbor, anthropology, is its interest in the *regularities* in human conduct and the *overall patterns* of social change. This interest is reflected in the methods used by sociologists in their work. Taking their cue from the procedures of the natural sciences, sociologists often begin by examining contemporary or historical societies in order to form general hypotheses to account for personal behavior and social change. These general theories are then tested against additional historical data or, more commonly, against contemporary data gathered for this purpose through interviews and statistical surveys. The results of the tests lead to the acceptance, rejection, or modification of the hypotheses. Throughout the process the emphasis remains on the theory being tested. Individual pieces of data are of interest only insofar as they confirm or deny the overall theory. Because of this emphasis on theories and patterns, the sociological method is most effective in dealing with recurring behavior and values and with social phenomena found regularly in a number of different societies. The method is least effective in dealing with unique or rare phenomena that depart from the expected norm. In practice this means that sociology is a generalizing science.[3] Sociologists tend to operate at a fairly high

---

2. Bert F. Hoselitz, ed. *A Reader's Guide to the Social Sciences*, rev. ed. (New York: Free Press, 1970), p. 1. All subsequent references are to the revised edition.
3. This point was emphasized strongly by Max Weber (*The Methodology of the Social Sciences*, ed. and trans. E. A. Shils and H. A. Finch [New York: Free Press, 1949]; *Basic Concepts in Sociology*, trans. H. P. Secher [Secaucus, N. J.: Citadel Press, 1980], pp. 29-55). Cf. Emile Durkheim, *The Rules of Sociological Method*, 8th ed., trans. S. A. Solovay and J. H. Mueller and ed. G. E. G. Catlin (New York: Free Press, 1964); and Hoselitz, *Reader's Guide*, pp. 1-17.

level of abstraction and to deal with general types of social phenomena, specific examples of which can be found in a number of individual societies. They tend to neglect unique phenomena that cannot be absorbed into a more general "ideal type."

Modern sociology's stress on general social patterns and theories is part of its inheritance from the early social theorists and can be seen most clearly in the work of the founders of the discipline, many of whom remain highly influential. Because of their importance for biblical studies, four of these—Herbert Spencer, Karl Marx, Max Weber, and Emile Durkheim—deserve special attention.

Herbert Spencer

Herbert Spencer (1820-1903) is best known as a proponent of Social Darwinism, an evolutionary theory of society that had an enormous influence on social scientists and eventually on students of Israelite religion. Drawing on Charles Darwin's influential work on the origin of species through natural selection, Spencer held that all societies undergo an inevitable evolutionary development. As small homogeneous societies increase in size, there is more competition for goods and services, a situation that leads to social unrest, which is eventually resolved by increased specialization and enforced co-operation. If military force plays a role in this process, small groups must combine into larger ones for mutual protection, and the social differentiation process continues. Eventually industrialized societies can arise, but these too have their own evolutionary patterns that insure the "survival of the fittest." Although Spencer's work seems to have had no direct influence on biblical studies, the general model of social change that he advocated and his notion that all things inevitably evolve from the simple to the complex are typical of the sort of evolutionary perspective still found in some treatments of Israelite religion and literature.[4]

Karl Marx

The work of Karl Marx (1818-1883) is normally associated with political science and economics, but in fact his voluminous writings embrace all of the social sciences. Early in his career he was influenced by Hegel's philosophy of history, which saw history

---

4. Herbert Spencer, *First Principles*, 6th ed. (London: Williams & Norgate, 1928); *The Principles of Sociology*, 3d ed. (New York: Appleton, 1900). For a brief discussion of the work of Darwin and Spencer, see Abram Kardiner and Edward Preble, *They Studied Man* (New York: Mentor, 1963), pp. 15-49.

ideologically as a dialectical process moving from thesis through antithesis to synthesis. However, Marx later became sharply critical of this position and argued that the forces underlying historical change are economic and social rather than ideological. Marx saw history as a series of interactions between different social groups, each having particular economic interests. Social systems containing such divergent groups are basically unstable, and this instability is increased as technology develops. A society's technological resources are at the disposal of the ruling class, which is therefore able to control the society's means of production and to exploit the working classes (the proletariat). The ruling class seeks to perpetuate this situation and actively opposes social change, often by using increasingly harsh means of repression. In contrast, the working classes, once they recognize their exploitation, seek to reverse their oppression and eventually revolt. The revolution leads to alterations in the social structure and permits the development of new technology, and the whole cycle is repeated. Marx illustrated this process by showing that capitalism arose only after the overthrow of feudalism made possible the full development of the Industrial Revolution. He further predicted that the oppressed workers of his own day would eventually recognize their situation and overthrow the capitalist system.[5]

Since Marx's death, many parts of his highly complex system have been called into question, either by the course of historical events or by the work of later scholars. Still, his general point of view has been enormously influential. His stress on the economic and social dimensions of historical change has caused many historians to alter the focus of their history writing and to examine more closely the economic structure of the societies they are studying. Although Marxist theory has only recently had an effect on the study of ancient Israelite religion, some biblical scholars have begun to take seriously Marx's basic notion that historical forces are essentially social and economic in character and can be uncovered through social scientific investigation.[6]

5. Karl Marx's thought cannot easily be summarized because of its enormous extent and complexity. His most comprehensive work, *Das Kapital*, was published in three volumes (1867–94) and is available in a number of English translations. See, for example, *Capital*, ed. Frederick Engels, 3 vols. (New York: International Publisher, 1967). For a brief introduction to Marx's sociological thought, together with a useful collection of his writings on the subject, see Neil J. Smelser, *Karl Marx on Society and Social Change* (Chicago: University of Chicago Press, 1973).

6. See, for example, Norman K. Gottwald, *The Tribes of Yahweh* (Maryknoll, N. Y.: Orbis Books, 1979). For an early attempt to apply Marxian analysis to the Old Testament, see M. Lurje, *Studien zur Geschichte der wirtschaftlichen und sozialen Verhältnisse im israelitisch-jüdischen Reiche* (Giessen: Alfred Töpelmann, 1927).

Max Weber

In opposition to Marx's dialectical materialism, Max Weber (1864-1920) held that history is shaped not by economic interests but by a society's commonly held value orientations. He thus sought to explain the advent of capitalism by correlating its appearance with the rise of Calvinism, which considered disciplined conduct and hard work to be moral and religious values. To test this thesis, he studied in detail the value systems of ancient and modern societies outside of Europe and concluded that capitalism did not arise in any of them because the requisite value systems were not present.[7]

Although Weber's basic thesis did not influence biblical scholarship significantly, one of the studies that he undertook in order to test his theory made a lasting imprint on Old Testament research. As part of his examination of non-European societies he made a detailed examination of ancient Israel, the first such study to be produced by a modern sociologist.[8] Basing his work on the critical Old Testament scholarship of his day, Weber held that early Israel was an uneasy amalgamation of seminomadic and settled agricultural groups that were occasionally unified politically in times of crisis by means of a covenant. By holding in common the religious ideal of the covenant, the groups were able to rise above their individual economic interests and join together in a military league for the common good. In this early period Israel had no permanent political system but was governed from time to time by "charismatic" leaders, people believed to be endowed with exceptional or even supernatural powers that were of divine origin and that set them apart from normal human beings. This situation began to change with the rise of the monarchy, when the traditional political system was gradually replaced by one inspired by the Canaanites. Economic and political power began to accumulate in the hands of wealthy landowners, who increasingly oppressed the remainder of the population. On religious and ethical grounds the prophets opposed this abuse of power and lamented the disappearance of the equality inherent in Israel's traditional system. The prophetic stress on ethical behavior motivated by a desire to fulfill the covenant by obeying the divine will eventually reemerged in Calvinism.[9]

7. Max Weber, *The Protestant Ethic and the Spirit of Capitalism* (New York: Charles Scribner's Sons, 1930); *The Theory of Social and Economic Organization* (New York: Oxford University Press, 1947); Hoselitz, *Reader's Guide*, pp. 12-14.

8. Max Weber, *Ancient Judaism* (New York: Free Press, 1952).

9. Weber, *Ancient Judaism*, pp. 3-335; Herbert F. Hahn, *The Old Testament in Modern Research*, expanded ed. (Philadelphia: Fortress Press, 1966), pp. 159-65.

Weber's treatment of Israelite history and religion made an immediate impression on Old Testament scholarship, and many of his theories remain highly influential. However, equally important were his contributions toward a definition of the emerging discipline of sociology. Although the tendency to generalize had been a characteristic of sociology from the beginning, Weber gave this tendency a clear methodological role. He held that sociology is preeminently a generalizing science and that sociologists test their hypotheses by ignoring the unique features of the objects of study and by concentrating instead on general characteristics. This emphasis on generalization can bring the sociologist into direct conflict with the historian, who is interested in the particulars of a society, and can raise serious methodological problems for biblical scholars who want to apply sociological methods to the study of ancient Israel.[10]

Emile Durkheim

Like his contemporary, Max Weber, Emile Durkheim (1858-1917) was not only an original social theorist but also a major force in shaping sociological method. He insisted that the various sociological components of a culture are organically interrelated and have a direct impact on individuals within the culture. Social forces in a sense are external to individuals and are only secondarily internalized so that they shape human character. Because these forces have an independent existence, both in their own right and as part of the whole society, they can rightly be considered "facts" and may be studied by the same scientific methods that are applied to physical "facts." In order to understand any society, then, it is necessary to study its sociological components and the way they interact to influence individual behavior.

Durkheim's view of society as an organism having a number of interacting parts had a profound effect on later sociological research and was one of the inspirations for the functionalist approach to anthropology. His work has had little direct influence on Old Testament studies, but his concepts of society and the nature of social forces lie behind many of the recent attempts to study ancient Israelite society as an integrated whole.[11]

10. Weber, *Methodology; Basic Concepts*, pp. 29-55. For a discussion of Weber's influence on Old Testament studies, see Hahn, *Old Testament in Modern Research*, pp. 165-76; and Jay A. Holstein, "Max Weber and Biblical Scholarship," *HUCA* 46(1975):159-79.

11. Emile Durkheim, *Rules of Sociological Method; The Elementary Forms of the Religious Life* (New York: Free Press, 1947); Hoselitz, *Reader's Guide*, pp. 15-17; Kardiner and Preble, *They Studied Man*, pp. 95-116.

Anthropology

Anthropology, broadly defined, is the study of all facets of human life and culture and deals with questions of human origins, social organization, customs, folklore, and beliefs. Because of its broad interests, anthropology sometimes overlaps with the other social sciences, particularly sociology. However, at least in the twentieth century, anthropology has generally not shared sociology's interest in overarching theories but has tended to concentrate on the analysis of particular societies and cultural phenomena, especially those that differ from what is normally found in the industrialized West. In the United States it is common to divide the discipline into two major areas of research: physical anthropology and cultural anthropology. Physical anthropology is concerned with human origins and with the physiological links between various types of modern humans and earlier hominids. Cultural anthropology considers all aspects of society and culture and embraces a number of subfields, among which are ethnology, social anthropology, ethnography, archaeology, and structural anthropology. The boundaries between these subfields are not always well marked, and it is fairly common for individual anthropologists to move freely from one area of study to another.[12] Because of the important role that these subfields have played in Old Testament research, it will be helpful to consider each of them briefly in order to understand their distinctive interests and methods.

Ethnology

Ethnology is the "theoretical and comparative study of human custom" and has roots that stretch back to the beginnings of western intellectual history.[13] The first ethnologists were travelers and explorers, who brought back to their own cities strange tales of the curious people and customs encountered during their journeys. Such travelers' reports were compiled even in antiquity, but they began to appear in increasingly large numbers during the age of exploration that followed the waning of the Middle Ages. By the nineteenth century a considerable amount of comparative data had accumulated, and anthropologists began to synthesize this material in theoretical discussions of various aspects of culture. Many, although

---

12. Hoselitz, *Reader's Guide*, pp. 41–47; J. W. Rogerson, *Anthropology and the Old Testament* (Atlanta: John Knox Press, 1979), pp. 9–10.
13. Hoselitz, *Reader's Guide*, p. 46.

not all, of these anthropological theorists were influenced by the same sort of evolutionism that pervaded the work of other social scientists of the period. Thus, for example, Johann Bachofen (1815–1887) attempted to trace the evolution of matriarchical societies into patriarchies, while Lewis H. Morgan (1818–1881) sketched the development of societies from "savagery" to "civilization."[14]

Particularly important because of its influence on Old Testament studies was the work of Edward B. Tylor (1832–1917), who outlined a theory of the evolution of human culture, paying special attention to the development of religious beliefs. Tylor's starting point was the observation that many civilized peoples have unusual beliefs and customs that seem to play no essential social role. He theorized that these anachronistic phenomena are in fact survivals from an earlier stage of cultural development. Such survivals not only demonstrate that the culture in which they are found evolved from an earlier, more primitive culture but also provide important clues to help the anthropologist reconstruct the past. Using this "doctrine of survivals," Tylor then turned his attention to an area of social life in which survivals are particularly noticeable, the area of religion and mythology. Employing large quantities of comparative data, he reconstructed the complex evolution of religious belief from simple primitive animism (the belief in a soul or spirit) through polytheism to monotheism, the form of religion found in "civilized" societies.[15]

Tylor's work immediately influenced Old Testament scholars, who quickly began to use the notion of cultural survivals to reconstruct early Israelite religion and culture. However, equally important was his influence on other anthropologists. The search for cultural survivals encouraged the collection of the religious beliefs of "primitive" societies and ultimately helped to establish comparative mythology and folklore studies as a subfield of ethnology. One of the early collections of this sort of material was made by James George Frazer (1854–1941), whose monumental work *The Golden Bough* drew together myths taken from a wide variety of ancient and modern sources. This material was set in the context of theories about "primitive mentality" and magic that bore a marked resemblance to

14. Johann J. Bachofen, *Das Mutterrecht* (1861; reprint, Basel: Schwabe, 1948); *Myth, Religion, and Mother Right: Selected Writings of J. J. Bachofen*, trans. Ralph Manheim (Princeton: Princeton University Press, 1967); Lewis H. Morgan, *Ancient Society* (New York: Henry Holt, 1878).

15. Edward B. Tylor, *Researches into the Early History of Mankind*, 3d ed. (London: John Murray, 1878; abridgement, ed. Paul Bohannan, Chicago: University of Chicago Press, 1964); *Primitive Culture* (London: John Murray, 1871); Kardiner and Preble, *They Studied Man*, pp. 50–68.

the developmental theories of Tylor.[16] Since the work of Frazer and the earlier pioneering collections of Jacob and Wilhelm Grimm, folklore studies has developed into a complex science with sophisticated methods for collecting and classifying folktales. Techniques of oral composition and transmission have been studied extensively, and tools have been developed to uncover the common literary structures of many of the stories.[17]

Although Tylor and the other evolutionists were influential in their own time, their theories have generally been rejected or greatly modified by contemporary anthropologists, who are normally unwilling to speak of inevitable evolutionary stages in human culture. However, modified evolutionary theories survive in some anthropological circles and have recently been advanced most forcefully by scholars interested in the ways in which small groups evolve into complex societies.[18]

Social Anthropology

Social anthropology, which is sometimes considered comparative sociology, is concerned with social organization rather than with social customs. The origins of this discipline lie in the attempts of nineteenth century anthropologists to describe kinship systems and the evolution of the family. Emile Durkheim played a prominent role in early social anthropology, but around the turn of the century the work of Bronislaw Malinowski (1884-1942) and A. R. Radcliffe-Brown (1881-1955) redefined the field in a dramatic way. Beginning with Durkheim's organismic view of society, Radcliffe-Brown argued that societies are best understood by conceiving them in

16. James George Frazer, *The Golden Bough*, 12 vols., 3d ed. (New York: Macmillan, 1935); *Folklore in the Old Testament*, 3 vols. (London: Macmillan, 1918). For an assessment of Frazer's work and its influence on Old Testament studies, see Kardiner and Preble, *They Studied Man*, pp. 69-94; Rogerson, *Anthropology*, pp. 22-65; and Hahn, *Old Testament in Modern Research*, pp. 53-59.

17. For a survey of the influence of folklore studies on Old Testament research, see Rogerson, *Anthropology*, pp. 66-85. Among more recent studies, note particularly V. Propp, *Morphology of the Folktale*, 2d ed. (Austin: University of Texas Press, 1968); Alexander H. Krappe, *The Science of Folklore* (1930; reprint, New York: W. W. Norton, 1964); Robert C. Culley, *Studies in the Structure of Hebrew Narrative* (Philadelphia: Fortress Press, 1976); Albert B. Lord, *The Singer of Tales* (Cambridge, Mass.: Harvard University Press, 1960; reprint, New York: Atheneum, 1965); Ruth Finnegan, *Oral Literature in Africa* (Oxford: At the Clarendon Press, 1970); *Oral Poetry* (New York and Cambridge: Cambridge University Press, 1977).

18. See, for example, Leslie A. White, *The Evolution of Culture* (New York: McGraw-Hill, 1959); Julian H. Steward, *Theory of Culture Change* (Urbana: University of Illinois Press, 1955); Elman R. Service, *Primitive Social Organization: An Evolutionary Perspective* (New York: Random House, 1964); *The Origins of the State and Civilization: The Process of Cultural Evolution* (New York: W. W. Norton, 1975); Morton H. Fried, *The Evolution of Political Society* (New York: Random House, 1967); Marshall D. Sahlins and Elman R. Service, ed., *Evolution and Culture* (Ann Arbor: University of Michigan Press, 1960).

biological terms. Just as a biological organism consists of interacting parts which together form an integrated whole, so a society consists of individuals and groups tied together by social relations. These interacting social units form the structure of the society, and one may then speak either of the functioning of the society's structure or of the function of any particular part in relationship to the whole.[19]

Radcliffe-Brown's functionalist approach not only made a lasting impact on anthropological theory but also had important implications for the way that social anthropologists went about their task. Because societies were seen as organic units composed of a number of interrelated parts, social phenomena could no longer be considered in isolation. Rather, the phenomena had to be studied in their sociological context and then analyzed so as to show their function in the society as a whole. Whereas earlier anthropologists such as Tylor and Frazer had abstracted data from a number of societies and then incorporated the data in a theoretical interpretive schema, Radcliffe-Brown and his followers stressed the importance of studying whole societies in detail. This shift in emphasis helped to correct some of the methodological weaknesses in the older approach, but the functionalist position was itself vulnerable to criticism because it tended to see societies as static systems and had difficulty dealing with social change. Yet in spite of this problem, which is inherent not in the functionalist approach itself but in the application of that approach, Radcliffe-Brown's views dominated social anthropology for many years, particularly in Great Britain, while his stress on social function and his insistence on the necessity of doing intensive fieldwork in order to understand a society have become important components of the general discipline of anthropology.[20]

Ethnography

Ethnography is simply the detailed description of individual cultures, normally by means of participant observation. Such descriptions are basic to all anthropological research, for they supply the raw data used by anthropologists to propound and test their hypotheses. Ethnographic research has been carried out

19. A. R. Radcliffe-Brown, "On the Concept of Function in Social Science," in his *Structure and Function in Primitive Society* (New York: Free Press, 1965), pp. 178–87.

20. For a survey of the history of social anthropology and a critical discussion of its methods, see E. E. Evans-Pritchard, "Social Anthropology," in his *Social Anthropology and Other Essays* (New York: Free Press, 1964), pp. 1–134; and Robert K. Merton, *On Theoretical Sociology* (New York: Free Press, 1967), pp. 78–138.

since antiquity, but only in the late nineteenth century did scholars begin to produce reliable, comprehensive accounts of individual societies.

Much modern ethnography is the work of functional anthropologists, whose interest in the functioning of the social structure requires the collection of information on all aspects of a society. Since A. R. Radcliffe-Brown's study of the Andaman Islanders in 1906 and Bronislaw Malinowski's study of the Trobriand Islanders in 1914, British anthropologists in particular have turned out a steady stream of detailed reports on individual societies, most of them proto-literate cultures that have relatively simple social systems. The studies of E. E. Evans-Pritchard on the Nuer, Paul and Laura Bohannan on the Tiv, Raymond W. Firth on the Tikopia, and Meyer Fortes on the Tallensi are classic examples of the results that can be achieved when anthropologists spend years living in a culture and keeping careful, systematic records on even the most insignificant details of its daily life. Comparative material of this type is especially valuable to Old Testament interpreters and historians attempting to set particular texts and cultural phenomena into a comprehensive social framework.[21]

Archaeology

Archaeology is the description and interpretation of the remains of past societies. When anthropologists undertake archaeological research, they are normally interested in the origin and development of various aspects of civilization in particular geographical areas. However, increasingly anthropologists are turning to archaeology in

21. For a survey of important ethnographic studies and indexes, see Hoselitz, *Reader's Guide*, pp. 80–90. Note particularly the following classic works: Franz Boas, *The Central Eskimo* (Washington, D.C.: U.S. Bureau of American Ethnology, 1888); Laura and Paul Bohannan, *The Tiv of Central Nigeria* (London: International African Institute, 1953); Frederick R. Eggan, *Social Organization of the Western Pueblos* (Chicago: University of Chicago Press, 1950); E. E. Evans-Pritchard, *The Nuer* (Oxford: At the Clarendon Press, 1940); Raymond W. Firth, *We, the Tikopia*, 3d ed. (Boston: Beacon Press, 1963); Meyer Fortes, *The Dynamics of Clanship Among the Tallensi* (London: Oxford University Press, 1945); *The Web of Kinship Among the Tallensi* (London: Oxford University Press, 1949); Melville J. Herskovits, *Dahomey*, 2 vols. (Locust Valley, N. Y.: J. J. Augustin, 1938); Henri A. Junod, *The Life of a South African Tribe*, 2d ed. (London: Macmillan, 1927); Clyde Kluckhohn, *Navaho Witchcraft* (Cambridge, Mass.: Harvard University Press, 1944); Hilda Kuper, *The Swazi* (London: International African Institute, 1952); Edmund R. Leach, *Political Systems of Highland Burma* (Cambridge, Mass.: Harvard University Press, 1954); Robert H. Lowie, *The Crow Indians* (New York: Farrar & Rinehart, 1935); Bronislaw Malinowski, *Argonauts of the Western Pacific* (London: Routledge & Kegan Paul, 1922); S. F. Nadel, *A Black Byzantium* (London: Oxford University Press, 1942); A. R. Radcliffe-Brown, *The Andaman Islanders* (Cambridge: At the University Press, 1922); Robert S. Rattray, *Ashanti* (Oxford: At the Clarendon Press, 1923); W. H. R. Rivers, *The Todas* (London: Macmillan, 1906); C. G. and Brenda Z. Seligman, *The Veddas* (Cambridge: At the University Press, 1911): W. Lloyd Warner, *A Black Civilization* (New York: Harper & Brothers, 1937); Monica Wilson, *Good Company: A Study of Nyakyusa Age Villages* (London: Oxford University Press, 1951).

21

order to reconstruct the social history of groups that are still in existence. Biblical scholars have traditionally made extensive use of archaeology, but only recently have they begun to explore the sociological implications of their data.[22]

Structural Anthropology

Structural anthropology is a fairly recent discipline, which is usually associated with the work of Claude Levi-Strauss. It attempts to apply to anthropological data the sorts of structuralist principles found in certain types of linguistic and literary analysis and is interested in making generalizations without repeating the methodological mistakes of nineteenth-century theoreticians. To date, Old Testament scholars have shown little interest in using anthropological structuralism, although they have begun to make extensive use of literary structuralism. However, a few structural anthropologists have used the method to throw new light on Israelite religion and culture, and it may be that in the future this type of structuralism will play a more significant role in biblical research.[23]

Psychology

Psychology is the social science that is concerned with the way in which mental states and processes are related to human behavior. Although psychologists have occasionally ventured into Old Testament interpretation, biblical scholars have generally avoided psychological approaches because of the methodological difficulties involved in doing this sort of analysis on historical figures. However, Old Testament critics have begun to use the work of social psychologists, whose research deals primarily with the sociological and psychological aspects of small groups and the individuals within them.[24]

22. For a survey of recent trends and studies in this area, see William G. Dever, "The Impact of the 'New Archaeology' on Syro-Palestinian Archaeology," *BASOR* 242(1981):15–29.

23. Literary structuralism does not concern us here. For examples of structuralist analyses of ancient Israelite religion and society, see Mary Douglas, *Purity and Danger* (London: Routledge & Kegan Paul, 1966), pp. 41–57; *Implicit Meanings* (London: Routledge & Kegan Paul, 1975), pp. 249–318; and Julian Pitt-Rivers, *The Fate of Shechem, or the Politics of Sex* (New York and Cambridge: Cambridge University Press, 1977), pp. 113–71. A critical evaluation of the structuralist approach is provided by Rogerson, *Anthropology*, pp. 102–19.

24. Hoselitz, *Reader's Guide*, pp. 26–30, 91–127.

THE USE OF THE SOCIAL SCIENCES
BY OLD TESTAMENT CRITICS

As we have already noted, research in the social sciences has often influenced Old Testament scholars, who have applied social scientific approaches both to the study of Israelite religion and to the study of biblical literature. This influence is most obvious in work done around the turn of the century, when a number of Old Testament critics used the rapidly emerging social sciences to supply new perspectives on traditional biblical problems. However, within a generation such experimental cross-disciplinary research was severely curtailed, and biblical scholars employed the social sciences primarily when they made comparative use of archaeological and ancient Near Eastern textual data. Only in recent years have scholars again begun to explore the ways in which social sciences other than archaeology might aid the Old Testament interpreter and historian. In order to understand the reasons for this unusual situation, it is necessary to examine in greater detail the ways in which early critical scholars used sociological approaches to study Israelite religion and literature and to see the methodological difficulties raised by such comparative work.

The Social Sciences and the Study
of Israelite Religion

Early Old Testament critics used both sociology and anthropology in order to elaborate the traditional picture of Israel's religion. As we have already noted, one of the early applications of a sociological approach was made not by a biblical scholar but by a sociologist, Max Weber. However, Old Testament critics were quick to follow Weber's lead, and his theories on early Judaism were applied in a number of studies of Israelite religion. Thus, for example, Adolphe Lods (1867–1948) wrote a history of Israel that amplified Weber's thesis that the early nomadic Israelite groups were in constant social conflict with the settled urban peoples of Canaan. The religious dimensions of this were further developed by Antonin Causse (1877–1947), who argued that in Israel's nomadic period religion and social structure were closely linked but that these links were broken after the tribes settled in Palestine. The resulting instability in Israelite society was of great concern to the prophets, who responded by advocating an individualistic notion of religion and society that stressed the importance of personal ethical behavior. Weber's influence is also noticeable in the work of Louis Wallis (b. 1876), who in a series of books tried to show the impact of social forces on Israelite religion by demonstrating that Hebrew monotheism grew out of an attempt to impose nomadic clan ethics on the urban Israelite state.[25]

Just as historians of Israelite religion used sociological theories, so they also made use of the anthropological data that was rapidly accumulating around the turn of the century. W. Robertson Smith (1846–1894) and Julius Wellhausen (1844–1918) both used Tylor's notion of "survivals" to argue that elements of early Semitic culture were still preserved in contemporary Arabic tribes and that these survivals could be employed along with classical Arabic texts to reconstruct the religion and society of ancient Israel. Frazer's mammoth collection of anthropological data was also used as a convenient source of survivals that could throw much needed light on obscure features of Israelite religion. Frazer himself made the first application of this material to the Old Testament, but other scholars soon joined him in pointing out parallels between ancient and modern religious phenomena.[26]

The Social Sciences and the Study of Israelite Literature

The social sciences began to play a major role in the study of Israelite literature with the work of Hermann Gunkel (1862–1932), whose form-critical approach was developed under the influence of nineteenth-century folklore studies. Gunkel maintained that every literary genre in the Old Testament had an original setting in Israel's national life (*Sitz im Volksleben*). In order to understand a genre, it was thus necessary to know the setting from which it came. Israelite literature could no longer be studied in isolation but had to be set in a specific social matrix, a task which could be facilitated through the use of the data being collected by folklorists and ethnographers.

Gunkel's insights were developed by a number of his disciples, who further refined his methods. Particularly important was the work of Sigmund Mowinckel (1884–1966), who stressed the importance of oral tradition in the formation of Israelite literature. Again relying on contemporary folklore studies, Mowinckel and his followers were able to demonstrate how oral literature is created, shaped, and

---

25. For a discussion of Weber's influence, see Hahn, *Old Testament in Modern Research*, pp. 165–84 and the literature cited there.
26. See Hahn, *Old Testament in Modern Research*, pp. 44–82 and the literature cited there.

preserved until it is finally recorded in writing. However, it should be noted that, after Gunkel, studies of literary genres and oral traditions concentrated increasingly on the social matrix of the *language* used in the biblical text and began to ignore the sociological role that literary genres played in Israelite life.[27]

The Rejection of Social Scientific Approaches

Even this brief description of how the social sciences were first used by Old Testament critics provides a ready explanation for the later rejection of this type of comparative approach. The early advocates of sociological approaches to the Old Testament were heavily dependent on the sociological and anthropological research of their day, and their work therefore shared all of the weaknesses of that research. Like the sociologists and anthropologists whose work they used, Old Testament critics often wrenched the comparative material out of its social context and then embedded it in a comprehensive social theory that was frequently dominated by an evolutionary perspective. The theory and its accompanying evidence were then imposed on the Old Testament, which was interpreted so as to produce the desired results. Social scientists themselves had already recognized the methodological dangers of working with general sociological theories, and the British functionalists in particular were well aware that much of the published ethnographic evidence was unsystematically gathered and therefore of questionable value. When biblical scholars finally began to recognize these problems, they reacted by curtailing their use of anthropological and sociological material. In the process they also rejected the real contributions that the social sciences had made to the study of Israelite religion and literature.[28]

The Social Sciences in Contemporary
Old Testament Scholarship

Although it is relatively easy to see why many of the early sociological approaches to the Old Testament were rejected, it is more difficult to account for the recent resurgence of interest in using sociology and anthropology in biblical studies. However, it is probable that a number of factors are at work. First, Old Testament

---

27. Hahn, *Old Testament in Modern Research*, pp. 119–56; Robert R. Wilson, *Prophecy and Society in Ancient Israel* (Philadelphia: Fortress Press, 1980), pp. 1–13.

28. For a detailed example of this process, see Robert R. Wilson, *Genealogy and History in the Biblical World* (New Haven, Conn.: Yale University Press, 1977), pp. 1–18.

scholars have become increasingly aware of the problems involved in trying to read any ancient text. As we have already seen, an informed reader of the Bible must do everything possible to understand the society that shaped the language, images, symbols, and concepts that an author uses in order to communicate. The social sciences deal precisely with this area of inquiry, so it is not surprising that Old Testament scholars have begun to explore ways in which social scientific insights might be made part of the interpretive process.

Second, there has been an increasing awareness that although Old Testament critics have not openly applied sociological approaches to their material, they have nevertheless made certain tacit assumptions about the nature of Israelite religion and society. These assumptions have influenced the interpretive process and therefore need to be exposed and examined in the interests of sound methodology.

Finally, since the turn of the century much new social scientific material has become available, and social scientists themselves have corrected many of the problems inherent in earlier research. These developments have encouraged Old Testament scholars to try once again to develop methodologically responsible ways of using the social sciences in biblical interpretation.

Because the social scientific study of the Old Testament is still in its infancy, it is difficult to see clear trends in this area of research. Scholars are currently trying a number of different approaches, and it is doubtful that a single method will predominate in the near future. For the purposes of discussion, it is sufficient to categorize recent research on the basis of the particular branch of the social sciences being used.

Sociological Approaches

Some Old Testament scholars have recently returned to the writings of the great sociological theorists and have attempted to apply this work to the reconstruction of Israelite religion and society. Well aware of the dangers of applying an abstract schema to the biblical texts, the modern practitioners of a sociological approach have been careful to balance social theory with a thorough examination of the textual evidence. Thus for example, Abraham Malamat has analyzed the Israelite judges as examples of Weber's charismatic individual, while Paul Hanson has drawn upon Weber, Mannheim, and Troeltsch in order to amplify his picture of the social and religious conflicts that led to the emergence of Israelite apocalyptic. Certainly the most ambitious application of sociological theory to the

Old Testament is to be found in Norman Gottwald's mammoth study of the social and political development of Israel during the pre-monarchical period. Making some use of Weber but taking most of his interpretive theory from Marx, Gottwald synthesizes a massive amount of textual and archaeological data to argue that Israel emerged from a peasants' revolt which was fueled by commitment to an egalitarian social system and a monotheistic faith.[29]

Outside of the realm of sociological theory, some Old Testament scholars have made extensive use of social psychology to analyze Israel's literature and religion. As representatives of this approach one should note Robert P. Carroll's application of cognitive dissonance theory to Old Testament texts describing prophetic conflict and David Petersen's use of role theory to analyze the various social functions of Israelite prophets.[30]

Anthropological Approaches

In recent years Old Testament scholars have used a variety of anthropological approaches in an attempt to shed new light on Israelite religion and literature. Folklore studies have continued to be a source of information on the nature of oral literature, and because of this new evidence form critics have had to revise some of their ideas about the way in which oral traditions are created. However, much recent research has been drawing on anthropological data not previously used in Old Testament interpretation. George Mendenhall and James Flanagan have used recent ethnological theories on state formation in attempts to reconstruct Israel's history before the monarchy became firmly established. Taking a different tack, Robert Wilson, Burke Long, and Thomas Overholt have used the work of British functional anthropologists and American Indian ethnographers to chart the history and social functions of Israelite prophecy. Functionalist data has also been used by Robert Wilson to study the form and function of the Old Testament genealogies.[31]

29. Abraham Malamat, "Charismatic Leadership in the Book of Judges," in *Magnalia Dei: The Mighty Acts of God*, ed. Frank M. Cross et al. (Garden City, N. Y.: Doubleday & Co., 1976), pp. 152–68; Paul D. Hanson, *The Dawn of Apocalyptic* (Philadelphia: Fortress Press, 1975); Gottwald, *Tribes*.

30. Robert P. Carroll, *When Prophecy Failed* (New York: Seabury Press, 1979); David L. Petersen, *The Roles of Israel's Prophets* (Sheffield, JSOT Press, 1981).

31. George E. Mendenhall, "Social Organization in Early Israel," in *Magnalia Dei*, pp. 132–51; James W. Flanagan, "Chiefs in Israel," *JSOT* 20(1981):47–73; Wilson, *Prophecy and Society*; Burke O. Long, "Social Dimensions of Prophetic Conflict," *Semeia* 21(1981):31–53; "Prophetic Authority as Social Reality," in *Canon and Authority*, ed. George W. Coats and Burke O. Long (Philadelphia: Fortress Press, 1977), pp. 3–20; Thomas W. Overholt, "The Ghost Dance of 1890 and the Nature of the Prophetic Process," *Ethnohistory* 21(1974):37–63; "Jeremiah and the Nature of the Prophetic Process," in *Scripture in History and Theology*, ed. Arthur L. Merrill and Thomas W. Overholt

METHODOLOGICAL PROBLEMS

It is clear that no matter how enticing the use of sociological approaches may be, Old Testament interpreters must avoid the sorts of methodological problems that plagued earlier research of this type. Although scholars are still debating the question of methodology, it is possible to suggest some guidelines to minimize the risks of using sociology and anthropology in Old Testament interpretation.[32]

First, the interpreter must be thoroughly familiar with the social scientific approaches being used and must be aware of their scope and limits. In the case of sociology, this means keeping in mind the generalizing character of the discipline and the difficulties that arise when sociology is used in the study of history. The theoretical tendencies of sociological research must be recognized and taken into account when assessing the results of any sociological interpretation of Israelite history or literature. In the case of anthropology, the interpreter must be aware of the particular interests of the various subfields of anthropology and their divergent methods. This is particularly important when the interpreter wishes to use anthropological research having an evolutionary or functionalist perspective, for both of these approaches can result in a tendentious or overly selective presentation of anthropological data.

Second, the interpreter must use only the work of competent social scientists. Obviously in order to make such an assessment it is necessary to rely on peer evaluation within the social-scientific community, but an attempt should be made to be sure that the scholars whose work is used are reliable. In the case of anthropological material, this means that Old Testament interpreters must rely on work done in the twentieth century.

Third, the interpreter must understand anthropological or sociological research in its own context before applying it to the study of ancient Israel. Fragments of a sociological theory cannot be extracted from their original matrix and used in a way that would distort the original theory. Bits of anthropological data cannot be taken out of

---

(Pittsburgh: Pickwick Press, 1977), pp. 129–50; "Commanding the Prophets: Amos and the Problem of Prophetic Authority," *CBQ* 41(1979):517–32; "Prophecy: The Problem of Cross-cultural Comparison," *Semeia* 21(1981):55–78; Wilson, *Genealogy and History.* For an evaluation of recent sociological approaches to the Old Testament, see Cyril S. Rodd, "On Applying a Sociological Theory to Biblical Studies," *JSOT* 19(1981):95–106; and Burke O. Long, "The Social World of Ancient Israel," *Int* 37(1982):243–55.

32. For an elaboration of these guidelines, see Wilson, *Genealogy and History*, pp. 11–18; and *Prophecy and Society*, pp. 15–16.

their original setting. In general one must be fair to the work of the social scientist whose research is being used.

Fourth, the interpreter who uses anthropological data must survey a wide range of societies that contain the phenomenon being studied. This will help the interpreter to avoid using atypical material for comparative purposes.

Fifth, the interpreter must be aware of any interpretive schemata that social scientists have used to present their data. Such schemata should normally be avoided unless the interpreter consciously decides to use them.

Finally, the interpreter must apply social-scientific material to the Old Testament in such a way that the text itself remains the controlling factor in the exegetical process. This rule must be followed whether the interpreter is concerned only with the exegesis of the text or is also interested in reconstructing Israelite history. The comparative material is simply used to form a hypothesis which is then tested against the biblical text. The exegesis of the text itself will confirm, disprove, or modify the hypothesis. In this way comparative data can be used to broaden the horizons of the interpreter by suggesting new hypotheses and to assess the value of hypotheses previously advanced.

With these guidelines in mind, we shall now turn to some examples of how anthropological material might be used to study Israelite history, literature, and religion. Although these examples will illustrate only one type of social scientific approach, they will still serve to indicate procedures that can be followed in all types of cross-cultural research and will clearly show the scope and limits of the method.

III

Reconstructing Israel's History: An Anthropological Perspective on Israelite Society in the Period of the Judges

THE NATURE OF THE PROBLEM

The period of the judges has been the subject of numerous studies by historians of ancient Israel. Yet in spite of all of this activity, there is still no scholarly consensus on the course of Israelite history from the conquest of Canaan to the rise of the monarchy. One of the reasons for this lack of consensus is the inability of historians to agree on the nature and development of Israel's social structure during this period. This issue is a crucial one, for the Bible often presents premonarchical history in terms of the fortunes and interactions of Israel's principal social units, the tribes. Within the tribal context all important activities are said to have taken place. Therefore, in order to write a political, economic, or religious history of Israel during the period of the judges, the historian must first understand Israel's social history—the nature and development of the tribal system. The historian's views on this issue will inevitably influence the interpretation of other historical data and will ultimately shape the reconstruction of many aspects of early Israelite history.

The task of understanding Israel's premonarchical social structure is complicated by the nature of the available evidence. Archaeological material on Israelite life during the eleventh and twelfth centuries is minimal, and the data that have been collected have often been synthesized and presented so as to speak to the problem of the nature of the Israelite conquest of Canaan rather than to the problem of the structure of Israelite society after the conquest. This paucity of extrabiblical evidence has forced historians to draw most of their material from the Old Testament itself. However, the biblical accounts of the period of the judges are not comprehensive, and the reliability of the material that does exist has been hotly debated.

On the surface, the Old Testament picture of Israel during this period seems straightforward and non-controversial. According to the Book of Judges, the invading Israelites succeeded in capturing much of the land of Canaan, leaving only a few isolated cities in the hands of the original inhabitants (Judges 1). After the conquest, the twelve tribes settled in the areas that had been alloted to them, but the people soon "did what was evil in the sight of the Lord" and began worshiping the gods of the Canaanites who remained in the land. God punished this faithlessness by giving Israel into the power of alien rulers who oppressed the people until they cried out for relief. In response to their pleas, God sent a deliverer, who liberated them from foreign domination and "judged" them for a period of years, during which the land "had rest." This cycle of apostasy, oppression, deliverance, and rest was repeated a number of times during the period of the judges, and much of the Book of Judges is devoted to stories of the exploits of Israel's deliverers (Judges 2—16). In the end, however, these divinely chosen leaders were unable to keep order among the tribes (Judges 17—21) or to curb the growing power of the Philistines. Only with the establishment of the monarchy under Saul and David was the Philistine threat contained and the rule of law established throughout the land (1 Samuel—2 Samuel 8).

Although the biblical picture of the period of the Judges does not preserve many details about Israel's political or social structure, the texts suggest that the people were organized as a group of twelve tribes that acted together politically and religiously as a single nation. Within the nation the tribes enjoyed equal political power and social status, and equality also seems to have characterized the relationships between individual Israelites. Throughout much of the period the nation as a whole was presided over by a series of "judges," who began their careers as military heroes resembling Weber's charismatic individuals and then became political leaders as a result of their success as warriors. They presumably attempted to maintain order in the land by enforcing the laws attached to the covenant between God and Israel and were in effect the primary source of governmental authority until they were replaced by genuine monarchs.

In spite of the plausibility of this picture of Israel's premonarchical social and political structure, Old Testament historians have long raised questions about the reliability of the biblical account. To begin with, all of the biblical evidence comes from a single source and is the work of the Deuteronomistic Historian, whose distinctive theological views pervade the narratives. Although old, traditional tales of individual heroes are clearly recognizable in the present text of

Judges, most scholars feel that the apostasy-oppression-deliverance-rest pattern was contributed by the Historian, who retrojected into the period of the judges the much later Deuteronomistic view of Israel as a unified nation characterized by a self-destructive tendency to worship foreign gods. If this analysis of Judges is correct, then the degree of national unity exhibited by premonarchical Israel remains an open question that cannot be resolved simply by appealing to the present biblical text. Furthermore, genuinely archaic texts, such as the "Song of Deborah" (Judges 5), suggest that wars and other political activities were carried out by a limited number of tribes and not by the whole nation, a suggestion that is reinforced by the fact that individual deliverers seem to have performed their military exploits in restricted geographical areas. If Judges 5 is an accurate reflection of the extent of intertribal political activities, then it is doubtful that the deliverers were the national leaders that the Deuteronomistic Historian claims them to have been, and the actual political and judicial role of these figures remains uncertain. Finally, the Historian's picture of the location of political and judicial power in the premonarchical period appears to be inconsistent or at least ambiguous. On the one hand, political power seems to lie with the tribes, which are capable of acting on their own in the best interests of the nation. On the other hand, political and judicial authority seems to reside with a single leader, who in some senses is a forerunner of later Israelite kings. Given the stories about the lack of social order at the time of the judges (Judges 17—21), some scholars suspect that the whole idea of a single political leader in this period is a retrojection from monarchical times and that in fact primary political and judicial authority remained with individual tribes. However, if this was the case, then the sudden transition from tribal rule to monarchy requires more explanation than is provided by the biblical writers.[1]

In the light of the limited amount of evidence available to historians of the premonarchical period and the questionable reliability of this data, it is not surprising that scholars have proposed several different theories about the social organization of early Israel, and these theories have in turn strongly influenced scholarly understandings of the political and religious systems. For a number of years, the most

1. For a brief critique of the historiographic value of the biblical texts, see John H. Hayes and J. Maxwell Miller, ed., *Israelite and Judean History* (Philadelphia: Westminster Press, 1977), pp. 285-93; A. D. Mayes, *Israel in the Period of the Judges* (Naperville, Ill.: Alec R. Allenson, 1974), pp. 84-105; and Roland De Vaux, *The Early History of Israel* (London: Darton, Longman & Todd, 1978), 2:683-93.

widely accepted picture of premonarchical Israelite society was the one proposed by Martin Noth. Noth began his reconstruction by arguing for the essential accuracy of the biblical references to twelve Israelite tribes organized as a single unit during the period of the judges. In order to understand more clearly the nature of this unity and the significance of the number twelve, he then compared Israel to the ancient Greek amphictyony, an association of twelve (or six) tribes that met regularly for cultic celebration at a central shrine. The number of tribes participating in the amphictyony was determined by the requirement that each tribe be responsible for maintaining the sanctuary for a period of one or two months every year. On the basis of this comparative evidence Noth suggested that Israel began as a six-tribe confederation which later expanded to form an amphictyony of twelve tribes. The Israelite amphictyony worshiped at a common shrine, which had as its principal cult object the sacred ark. The central sanctuary was first at Shechem (Joshua 24), but because the ark was moved from time to time, Israel worshiped at a succession of central shrines. During certain festivals each tribe was required to send a representative to the sanctuary (cf. Num. 1:5–16), and it is probable that matters of common interest were discussed at such times. Religious ceremonies were performed, although their precise nature is uncertain, and covenants were made and laws established. Amphictyonic legal matters were presided over by a single judge, who was Israel's only nationally recognized official during this period. The judges, whose names have been preserved in the lists of "minor judges" (Judg. 10:1–5; 12:7–15), were not responsible for the local administration of justice, which was in the hands of tribal elders, but were charged with proclaiming and enforcing the covenant law, which applied to the whole nation (cf. Exodus 20—23). When the covenant law was violated, all of the tribes acted together to punish the offender, and they also joined in military activities for the common good.[2]

On the surface, Noth's reconstruction of early Israelite society is a convincing one that seems to take into account most of the biblical evidence. In addition to providing external support for the traditional picture of early Israel as a religious association of twelve tribes, the amphictyonic hypothesis also helps to explain the apparent ease with which Israel made the transition from tribal confederation to

2. Martin Noth, *Das System der zwölf Stämme Israels* (Stuttgart: W. Kohlhammer, 1930); *The History of Israel* (New York: Harper & Brothers, 1958), pp. 85–108.

monarchical state. Even during the period when the tribe was the primary political unit, Israel recognized the necessity of religious and military unity and acknowledged the authority of a single official in matters of covenantal law. Such a system would not have been radically different from the later monarchical organization, in which the tribes were unified by their allegiance to the king, who was the primary source of judicial authority and the enforcer of divine law.

However, in spite of the attractiveness of Noth's position, many scholars now reject it because of serious flaws in his original argument. Reexamination of the comparative evidence used by Noth indicates that Greek amphictyonies were characterized by their members' common worship around a central shrine, not by the number of participants in the confederation. In Greece and Italy amphictyonies sometimes had seven, eleven, or twenty-three members rather than the twelve that Noth took to be the norm. Furthermore, Noth's analysis of the Israelite tribal lists is open to question, and these texts may not accurately reflect the tribal situation in the period of the judges. Finally, it cannot be demonstrated that Israel had a central sanctuary before the rise of the monarchy. If this crucial feature of an amphictyony did not exist in premonarchical Israel, then it is unlikely that the amphictyony did either.[3]

An alternative to Noth's hypothesis has recently been proposed by George E. Mendenhall. Rejecting the amphictyonic theory because in Greece the amphictyony was an urban phenomenon, Mendenhall sees early Israel as a federation of peasants who had revolted against the oppression of the Canaanite cities and joined together in a covenant with God. Genuine kinship played no role in the federation, which was united solely by the members' allegiance to a God who was Israel's only ruler. The people celebrated their unity by worshiping at a central shrine containing the ark of the covenant, and this common worship provided theological support for communal military activities against potential oppressors.[4]

This hypothesis avoids the major pitfalls of Noth's theory, although the existence of a central sanctuary remains a problem, but Menden-

---

3. Critiques of Noth's theory may be found in Hayes and Miller, *History,* pp. 299–308; Mayes, *Israel,* pp. 15–83; De Vaux, *History,* 2:695–743; C. H. J. De Geus, *The Tribes of Israel* (Assen: Van Gorcum, 1976); Otto Bächli, *Amphiktyonie im Alten Testament* (Basel: Friedrich Reinhardt Verlag, 1977); and Barnabas Lindars, "The Israelite Tribes in Judges," in *Studies in the Historical Books of the Old Testament,* ed. J. A. Emerton, VTSup 30 (Leiden: E. J. Brill, 1979), pp. 95–112.
4. Mendenhall, "Social Organization in Early Israel," in *Magnalia Dei,* pp. 132–51.

hall has been criticized because of his insistence that the covenant was the sole basis of early Israelite unity and because of his claim that the formation of the nation was the result of a peasants' revolt.[5] Furthermore, Mendenhall's description of the covenant federation leaves unanswered a number of questions about the sources of political and judicial authority in early Israel. The theological claim that God was Israel's only ruler does not help to solve the problem of how the people actually enforced their laws. If early Israel was in fact a heterogeneous collection of peasants who had freed themselves from the oppression of the Canaanite cities, then the issue of judicial authority must have been a major one in the newly formed Israelite federation, and as a practical matter the people would have been encouraged to devise a political system capable of dealing with the problem. Finally, Mendenhall's hypothesis does not explain the reasons for Israel's transition from tribal federation to monarchical state. If the rationale for early Israel's existence was the rejection of the hierarchically organized Canaanite city-states and their rulers, then the people's sudden willingness to create their own monarchy is difficult to understand.

Recognizing some of the difficulties with Mendenhall's views, Norman K. Gottwald has proposed a more detailed reconstruction that accepts Mendenhall's peasant-revolt model of the formation of Israel but stresses the sociopolitical dimensions of the process. According to Gottwald, early Israelites were organized as egalitarian social units similar to bands or tribes. These bands were unified by their common worship of the God El, but they cooperated with each other politically only when they were threatened militarily. Their egalitarian social structure attracted peasants seeking to escape the oppression of the Canaanite city-states, and the size and political power of the bands began to increase. Eventually they were joined by groups that had experienced the exodus from Egypt and that testified to the power of Yahweh, the God who had freed the Hebrew slaves. The ideology of the exodus groups helped to give religious expression to the unity of early Israel, and the worship of Yahweh, now identified with El, became a central feature of the rapidly growing

---

5. Manfred Weippert, *The Settlement of the Israelite Tribes in Palestine* (Naperville, Ill.: Alec R. Allenson, 1971), pp. 55–126; J. Maxwell Miller, "Approaches to the Bible through History and Archaeology: Biblical History as a Discipline," *BA* 45(1982):214–16; Alan J. Hauser, "Israel's Conquest of Palestine: A Peasants' Rebellion?" *JSOT* 7(1978):2–19; Thomas L. Thompson, "Historical Notes on 'Israel's Conquest of Palestine: A Peasants' Rebellion?'" *JSOT* 7(1978):20–27; Philip J. King, "The Contribution of Archaeology to Biblical Studies," *JSOT* 45(1983):5–11.

Israelite coalition. As more Canaanite peasants joined the coalition, Israel became more diverse but also more powerful militarily and was finally able to curb the power of most of the local rulers and take control of the land. Israel in the period of the judges was thus a heterogeneous coalition of Hebrews and Canaanites who were unified by their common opposition to Canaanite imperialism. This ideological unity was undergirded by the cult of Yahweh, which supported political and economic equality at the individual and tribal levels. Most leadership positions were temporary, and the few hereditary offices that did exist were limited in scope. The primary social units were extended families, which were usually based on actual kinship, and village protective associations that gathered together extended families living in the same geographical area. Larger social groups, such as the tribe and the nation of Israel itself, usually functioned politically only in military contexts.[6]

Even though Gottwald's reconstruction still leaves unanswered the question of why the Israelites ultimately rejected their egalitarian society and placed themselves under the control of the same sort of monarchical state that they had fought so hard to destroy, his work provides the most sophisticated picture of early Israel available to date and must be the starting point for all future historical research. It is unlikely that a radically different reconstruction can be made without the discovery of additional extrabiblical evidence, but it may be possible to test and perhaps to modify or refine Gottwald's work by applying a different sort of sociological approach to the problem. However, in the interests of sound methodology, any reexamination of the issue must begin not with a critique of Gottwald's reconstruction of Israel's premonarchical social structure but with a survey of the available biblical and extrabiblical evidence on the history of this period. It is necessary to begin at this point for two reasons. First, any successful reconstruction of early Israelite history must take into account all of the biblical and extrabiblical data. Any reconstruction which does not do this will be suspect. Second, the nature of the available historical evidence may help to determine which type of sociological approach is likely to yield the most useful results and which types of comparative data are actually relevant to the evidence that already exists. As we have already noted, most of the historical evidence on the period of the judges comes from the biblical text itself, but some account must be taken of the existing archaeological material.

6. Norman K. Gottwald, *Tribes*, pp. 293–621.

The Biblical Evidence

Although scholars have persistently questioned some aspects of the Old Testament's picture of premonarchical Israel, they generally feel that several broad features of Israelite society can be reconstructed safely from the biblical text. First, it is clear that Israelites both before and after the conquest of Canaan organized themselves into relatively large groups traditionally called "tribes."[7] According to biblical tradition, the tribes were in existence as early as the ancestral period and persisted during the wilderness wanderings and the settlement of Canaan. The organizational structure of the tribes is often described by using the language of kinship. The founders of the twelve tribes of Israel are thus said to have been brothers, the sons of the same father (Jacob/Israel). Subdivisions of the tribes are similarly seen as the "children" of the tribal ancestors, and the whole social structure can be outlined as a branched genealogy having several levels (see, for example, Gen. 46:8–27; Exod. 6:14–25; Num. 26:5–62).

Second, premonarchical Israelite society seems to have had five levels, with each level containing increasingly large groups (cf. Judg. 7:16–18; 1 Sam. 10:20–21). At the lowest level of the social structure were individual nuclear families composed of parents, their unmarried children, and possibly one or more grandparents. The unity of the nuclear family was based on genuine kinship. At the next level of the social structure, several related nuclear families could form an extended family, usually referred to as a "father's house" (bêt- ʾab). This group too seems to have been based on genuine blood relationships and was composed of three or four generations of kin who traced their genealogies to a common ancestor four or five generations removed from the youngest members of the family. The size of an extended family would have depended on the number of nuclear families within it, but a group of fifty to one hundred people is a good estimate. Extended families could in turn join together to form a larger group, traditionally though inaccurately called a "clan" (mišpāḥāh). Although it is possible that the clan was composed of genuine kin, it is more likely that its unity was based on geographical proximity or common interests. In fact the clan may have corresponded to a single village or to a group of extended families that banded together for mutual protection. At the next stage, several clans could join to form a tribe. As in the case of the clan, the Old

7. For a dicussion of the problems raised by using the term "tribe" to refer to Israel's largest social group, see Gottwald, *Tribes*, pp. 293–98.

Testament sees kinship as the basis of tribal unity, but it is more likely that clans formed themselves into tribes for various reasons, including geographical proximity, common religious and cultural experience, and the need for more military protection than a single clan could provide. Finally, the twelve Israelite tribes formed the nation of Israel, the largest Israelite social unit mentioned in the Old Testament.[8]

Third, the tribes of Israel are said to have occupied specific geographical areas over which they had political control (Joshua 13—22; Judges 1). We do not need to be concerned here with the precise boundaries of the tribes or the exact locations of their cities. It is sufficient to note that boundaries seem to have been fairly rigid in the sense that members of one tribe did not routinely take up residence in another tribe's territory.

Fourth, the tribes are described as acting together for the common good, particularly in military and ritual contexts. At the same time, national unity did not always prevail, and there are indications of tensions between clans and tribes. These tensions sometimes led to hostility and armed conflict (Judg. 5:14-18; 17:1—21:35).

Fifth, no matter what Israel considered to be the basis of law in this period, legal decisions were difficult to enforce, particularly at the level of the clan or tribe (Judges 20—21). There seems to have been some truth in the Deuteronomistic Historian's comment that, "in those days there was no king in Israel; every man did what was right in his own eyes" (Judg. 21:25).

Finally, the texts mention a number of individual leaders, ranging from "elders" of the people to the judges themselves. The latter figures seem to have functioned primarily in military contexts, but when they did so they were dependent on the militias of the individual tribes and had no troups or special weapons of their own.

The Archaeological Evidence

Archaeologists writing on the period of the judges have traditionally used their evidence primarily to elucidate the Israelite conquest of Canaan. However, in recent years several Iron Age I (ca. 1200-1000 B.C.) sites have been surveyed or excavated, and scholars have begun to sketch the implications of this new material for our understanding of Israel's premonarchical social structure. A detailed reconstruction of early Israelite society must await the publication of

---

8. The various levels of Israelite society have been discussed in detail by Gottwald, *Tribes*, pp. 239-92.

considerably more data, both from new excavations and from completed excavations whose results are still unpublished. However, the general outlines of a tentative reconstruction are already beginning to emerge.[9]

Most of the sites that were occupied during the period of the judges appear to have been unfortified villages with economies based on farming or a combination of farming and herding. Agriculture must have been fairly well developed, for there is evidence of agricultural terraces, rock-cut cisterns, and storage pits. Several of the villages (for example, Tel Masos, Tel Esdar, Ai, and Izbet Sartah) contain early examples of the Israelite "four-room house," which consists of a long back room and two side rooms surrounding a central courtyard. At a typical site such as Tel Masos, these houses are between seventy-two and ninety-six square meters in area and are not physically connected with each other in any way. By applying standard formulas for calculating the number of people that can be housed in a given floor area, it can be determined that each of these dwellings sheltered six or seven people. An exception to this pattern may be found at Khirbet Raddana, where there are compounds consisting of four standard living units joined by a protective wall. At some sites cisterns are connected with individual houses, and there are also indications that the living units were used to store grain and even to shelter livestock. Although most of the four-room houses are roughly the same size, at Tel Masos one of the dwellings contains twice the normal amount of floor space. In this unit excavators also found pottery and artifacts that are not typical of those found in the other houses in the village.

This admittedly meager evidence suggests that in most Israelite villages the basic social unit was the nuclear family, which occupied a single dwelling. Each household seems to have been economically self-sufficient, collecting its own water, raising and storing its own grain, and keeping its own animals. Such an arrangement implies that each nuclear family also had exclusive rights to a certain amount of farm land, although there is no archaeological evidence to support this conclusion. In most villages extended families have left no traces of their existence, unless we are to assume that the village itself represented a single extended family. This assumption is unlikely, given the large size of some of the villages. It is probably therefore

9. For a convenient summary of the archaeological evidence, see King, "Archaeology," pp. 6–11; Frank S. Frick, "Religion and Sociopolitical Structure in Early Israel: An Ethno-archaeological Approach," *SBLSP* 1979, 2:233–53; and Y. Shiloh, "The Four-Room House—Its Situation and Function in the Israelite City," *IEJ* 20(1970):180–90.

safe to conclude that the extended family did not play the important social role that scholars have often attributed to it. An exception may be found at Khirbet Raddana, where the existence of housing compounds may indicate that extended families had greater social importance.

In most of the villages there are no indications of a hierarchical political structure, and in fact the apparent self-sufficiency of each household suggests that nuclear families received minimal benefit from the village in which they lived. Villages could supply a certain amount of protection, although the absence of fortifications suggests that defense was not a major problem during this period. Only in relatively large sites, such as Tel Masos, are there indications of the sort of social stratification that might indicate the presence of a central political leader such as a chief. The existence of an unusually large house at Tel Masos suggests that this particular village may have been developing a hierarchical political system.

THE CHOICE OF
AN ANTHROPOLOGICAL APPROACH

Both the biblical evidence and the archaeological data suggest that our picture of premonarchical Israel can best be elaborated by using comparative material drawn from anthropological studies of societies having a social structure based on real or fictitious kinship. In fact there are a number of modern examples of such societies, usually called *lineage systems* by anthropologists, and a great deal is known about the way in which these systems function. A comprehensive examination of lineage systems reveals that although each of them possesses some unique characteristics they also share many structural features. The existence of these common features in a large number of societies means that it is safe to make some generalizations about lineage structure and development.

A SURVEY OF
THE ANTHROPOLOGICAL EVIDENCE

The Nature of Lineages

Lineages use the concept of kinship as their fundamental organizational principle and are based on the model of the nuclear family.[10] At

10. I have discussed the features of lineages in detail in Wilson, *Genealogy and History*, pp. 18–37, where detailed bibliographical citations may be found. The following general discussions of lineage systems are particularly important: Max Gluckman "Introduction" to J. C. Mitchell and J. A. Barnes, *The Lamba Village* (Cape Town: University of Cape Town, 1950), pp. 1–19; John Middleton and David Tait, "Introduction" to *Tribes without Rulers*, ed. John Middleton and David Tait

the lowest structural level, the minimal lineage, the lineage group (sometimes also called a unilineal descent group) includes all of the children, male or female, that claim descent from the same parent. In minimal lineages only two generations of kin are involved, but two or more minimal lineages can be related to each other if they trace their ancestry to a single figure in the third generation. The larger lineage thus created can in turn be seen as part of a still larger lineage, in which all of the component lineages share an ancestor in the fourth generation. At least in theory, this process could be carried on indefinitely. Increasingly large groups would be formed as lineage members traced their ancestry to ever more remote figures, and by this process the whole society would come to resemble a hierarchy of nesting lineages. However, in practice even the largest lineages rarely claim descent from ancestors who are more than ten to twelve generations removed from the youngest members of the society. This self-imposed limit on the depth of the lineage also has the effect of setting rough limits on the size of the lineage. If the number of people in the lineage exceeds these limits, then it risks becoming socially unstable.

It is important to notice that the various levels of a complex lineage may not be equally important or have the same degree of social reality. Thus, for example, everyday economic and political activities usually take place at the lower levels of the social structure and involve small lineage groups such as nuclear or extended families. Larger lineage groups play little role in these activities but may become important on ritual occasions or in times of war, when small groups are incapable of defending the society. In a sense, then, these larger lineage groups function only on an occasional basis when their existence is made necessary by specified social conditions.

Lineages are not simply conceptual systems that help societies to understand and express social groupings based on a number of complex factors. On the contrary, lineages are concrete physical realities in the sense that they correspond to groups of people living in

(London: Routledge & Kegan Paul, 1958), pp. 1–31; M. Fortes and E. E. Evans-Pritchard, "Introduction" to *African Political Systems*, ed. M. Fortes and E. E. Evans-Pritchard (London: Oxford University Press, 1940), pp. 1–23; Meyer Fortes, "The Structure of Unilineal Descent Groups," *AA* 55(1953):17–41; M. G. Smith, "On Segmentary Lineage Systems," *JRAI* 86/2(1956): 39–80; Meyer Fortes, *Kinship and the Social Order* (Chicago: Aldine, 1969); Morton H. Fried, "The Classification of Corporate Unilineal Descent Groups," *JRAI* 87(1957):1–29; and Marshall D. Sahlins, "The Segmentary Lineage: An Organization of Predatory Expansion," *AA* 63(1961):322–45. For detailed analyses of individual societies organized by means of lineage systems, see Evans-Pritchard, *The Nuer*; Meyer Fortes, *The Dynamics of Clanship among the Tallensi* (London: Oxford University Press, 1945); and Meyer Fortes, *The Web of Kinship among the Tallensi* (London: Oxford University Press, 1949).

specific geographical areas. Lineage boundaries are also geographical boundaries, and as a result expansions and contractions of lineages are reflected geographically in the acquisition or abandonment of living space.

Because lineages use as their structural model the nuclear family, they are characterized by segmentation and may be represented by a branched or segmented genealogy, a "family tree." Just as the nuclear family can be seen both as a single cohesive unit and as a collection of unique individuals, so also lineage systems embody principles of unity and diversity, equality and inequality.

Individuals and groups in a lineage see themselves as a single social unit bound together by ties of actual kinship; geographical proximity; common culture, history, or religion; and political or economic interdependence. They perceive themselves to be a group over against other groups and sometimes celebrate their unity by engaging in common ritual activities. Outsiders share the lineage members' self-perception and view them as a corporate entity.

However, while lineages stress social cohesion, they also contain forces that press toward disunity and conflict. Such forces operate in both the horizontal and the vertical dimensions of the lineage. On the horizontal plane, individuals and lineage segments see themselves not only as part of a larger whole but also as independent entities in opposition to other independent entities on the same genealogical level. Such formal opposition has the potential to develop into actual social friction and ultimately into open conflict. On the vertical plane, the hierarchical character of lineages means that some individuals and groups are more powerful than others. Although people on the same genealogical level are theoretically equal to each other, they are inferior to those on higher levels. Lineages thus embody principles of inequality that must be regularized and controlled within the overall unity of the social system.

Because the stability of the social system depends on the lineage's being able to curb its natural tendency toward disunity, lineage societies have developed various ways of minimizing internal friction and settling disputes. This task is a difficult one, for political power resides in the lineage structure itself, and the few political leaders that do exist can exercise only the power that is delegated to them by the society's constituent elements. No single individual or group has enough power to solve disputes independently or to enforce legal decisions. For this reason conflicts within the lineage must be solved by means of a delicate series of negotiations.

The process by which lineages control divisive social forces can be seen most clearly in the hearings or "trials" that are held to adjudicate disputes between individuals and groups.[11] In the lower levels of large lineages, where group cohesion is based on actual kinship, judicial procedures are usually informal. In nuclear and extended families, the senior family member has sufficient authority to insure that the whole group conforms to the society's laws and customs. However, in the case of conflict between individuals or lineage segments that are related to each other by claiming descent from a fictitious or a dead ancestor rather than from a living one, the process is more complex. No living person is able to exercise authority over all of the disputants, so the conflict must be resolved voluntarily or mediated by people not directly involved. Unless a satisfactory solution can be found, the unity of the social structure will be jeopardized.

In typical cases of conflicts between individuals or lineage segments, the mediators are the heads or "elders" of other segments on the same genealogical level. The mediators have a delicate task, for the disputants often come to the hearing with groups of supporters from their own lineages, and as a result the society has already been partially polarized. If the elders try to impose a solution that is not acceptable to either of the two factions, then the dissatisfied lineage may withdraw from the society. Similarly, if the elders advocate a solution that does not seem fair to the other members of the society, then they will not bring to bear the social pressure necessary to enforce the decision. Both the disputants and the society at large must be satisfied if the conflict is to be resolved satisfactorily.

Most hearings begin when one individual or lineage segment lodges a complaint against another. In response to a direct request for a hearing, the elders must decide whether or not the matter is serious enough to warrant a public examination of the issues. If they feel that no wrong has actually been done or that the tension is not serious enough to cause major damage to the lineage, they will refuse to hear the complaint. On the other hand, if the elders feel that the conflict

11. For extensive discussions of lineage judicial procedures, together with numerous examples of individual cases, see Paul Bohannan, *Justice and Judgment among the Tiv* (London: Oxford University Press, 1957); Max Gluckman, *The Judicial Process among the Barotse of Northern Rhodesia* (Manchester: Manchester University Press, 1955); *The Ideas in Barotse Jurisprudence* (New Haven, Conn.: Yale University Press, 1965); P. H. Gulliver, *Social Control in an African Society* (London: Routledge & Kegan Paul, 1963); J. C. Vergouwen, *The Social Organization and Customary Law of the Toba-Batak of Northern Sumatra* (The Hague: Martinus Nijhoff, 1964); John Middleton, *Lugbara Religion* (London: Oxford University Press, 1960); and J. L. Messenger, "The Role of Proverbs in a Nigerian Judicial System," *SJA* 15(1969):64–73.

threatens the unity of the society or that a crime has actually been committed, they will hold a formal hearing at which the disputants and their supporters will be present. Hearings typically begin with references to the justness of the trial procedures and the fairness of the elders. Such references are also likely to appear during the hearing and are designed to convince the onlookers to accept the final verdict. To be sure, the elders are sometimes biased or even corrupt, but the ideal of justice must always be maintained in order for the judicial process to operate effectively.

The hearing process itself is usually a leisurely one. The elders are likely to know the facts of the case already, but both parties are allowed ample time to present their side of the issue. Witnesses may be called, and onlookers may informally volunteer useful information. The mediators themselves may ask questions in order to assure that all of the relevant evidence has been made public. When the elders feel that the problem has been discussed sufficiently, they render a decision. In the case of interpersonal disputes, they will propose a compromise which will be acceptable to both parties. If the elders are successful, then the unity of the lineage is restored.

In criminal cases, however, the procedure is more complex. The elders must not only determine guilt but also gather public support for the verdict. Without such support the society will not be willing to help enforce the penalties set by the court. The safest way for the elders to gain public support for a guilty verdict is to encourage the defendant to confess his guilt. If they are successful, then there is little chance that his supporters will challenge the verdict, and the elders can bring the proceedings to a close by prescribing punishment. Where the society has no set penalty for the crime, the elders must again negotiate a sentence which will be acceptable to everyone involved. Once this has been done, the judicial process ends, sometimes with a communal ritual stressing the renewed unity of the lineage.

Most lineage judicial procedures are viewed as strictly human processes. If the lineage's ancestral spirits or deities play any role at all, they simply serve as guarantors of the justness of the elders and the fairness of the hearings. Although mediums or diviners may help to determine whether or not a crime or an injury to the social structure has taken place, they are not likely to take part in the hearing itself. This is so because the involvement of the divine realm in the judicial process is likely to prevent the sort of negotiation that is essential to the successful resolution of lineage disputes. In cases where divination or oracles are used to determine guilt, the nature of the procedure insures that the defendant will be declared either guilty or innocent. There is no room for negotiated options, and the divine decision cannot be appealed. As a result, there is a greater likelihood of communal dissatisfaction with the verdict, especially if the society at large doubts the ability of the diviners.

The Growth and Disintegration of Lineages

Lineages grow naturally at their lower levels in two major ways. The most common source of lineage growth is the birth of children into the families of lineage members. However, equally important is the creation of nuclear families through marriage. Not only do these new minimal lineages add to the complexity of the society by providing the potential for lineage growth, but marriage may serve as a mechanism for incorporating outsiders into the lineage. Foreign individuals or groups may also be incorporated into the lineage by other means, and when the foreigners have been fully integrated they will be assigned an appropriate place in the lineage genealogy.

Similarly, lineages may dissolve because of the death of their members or because individuals or groups choose to leave the lineage for some reason. However, the major cause of lineage disintegration is the segmented structure of the lineage itself. At all levels there is a tendency for lineage segments to perceive their own unity in opposition to adjoining segments. This tendency is most noticeable at the lower levels of the lineage, where individuals and nuclear families are likely to be in frequent contact with each other and in competition for available land, resources, and services. The tensions caused by this competition sometimes grow into full-fledged disputes and threaten the unity of the lineage. Unresolved disputes may prompt dissident lineages to withdraw from the society and to join other groups, but we have already seen that low-level lineage tensions rarely reach this point. Because of kinship ties and the small number of people involved, negotiated settlements are usually able to prevent lineage disintegration. However, this is not the case at the upper levels of the lineage. When large lineage segments are in conflict, negotiation becomes more difficult because kinship bonds are weak or non-existent and because of the large number of divergent views that must be accommodated in any acceptable settlement. There is a greater possibility that judicial procedures will be ineffective, and for this reason the likelihood of lineage fission increases. Large lineages tend to be inherently unstable, and this tendency becomes stronger as the size and diversity of the overall lineage increases.

The Transition from Lineage to Monarchy

Lineage systems appear to be composed of structurally equal groups that govern themselves by means of a complex process of communal negotiation and consensus. Indeed, these systems have sometimes been characterized as "tribes without rulers," a description which implies that political hierarchies are incompatible with a lineage form of government.[12] In fact, such a view of the matter is oversimplified, for, as we have already noted, lineages also embody principles of inequality that can lead to the establishment of political elites. In lineages of any size, there are likely to be individuals who on the basis of age, social position, or specialized skills play leadership roles in certain specified contexts. So, for example, senior lineage members may represent their lineages at gatherings where rituals are performed, disputes settled, or political policy set. Individuals knowledgeable in tribal traditions may accumulate power by virtue of their ability to provide the lineage with crucial information. Skillful warriors may gain political influence by being chosen to lead the tribal militia. In societies where political policies and governmental decisions are made in individual lineages, these leadership roles are tightly controlled and may even be temporary or occasional. All leaders must still answer to their lineage constituencies. However, under certain conditions leaders can acquire enough power to transfer political authority from the lineages to a central government. An extreme form of such a central government is the monarchical state, in which all policy making and administration are located in the hands of a centralized bureaucracy under the control of a hereditary monarch. Access to leadership positions is strictly controlled, often by insisting that leaders come from particular families, and there is relatively little local political autonomy.

However, it is important to note that both the "pure" lineage government and the "pure" monarchical state are ideal types. Most actual governments are located somewhere between these two extremes.[13] So, for example, in a given society military power may be

---

12. Middleton and Tait, Tribes without Rulers; Fortes, "Structure," pp. 17–41.
13. Peter C. Lloyd, "The Political Structure of African Kingdoms," in Political Systems and the Distribution of Power (New York: Frederick A. Praeger, 1965), pp. 63–112; Lucy Mair, Primitive Government (Bloomington, Ind.: Indiana University Press, 1962).

centralized permanently or temporarily while judicial power remains in the hands of local lineages. In another society individual chiefs or kings may temporarily succeed in centralizing government functions because of a peculiar set of historical circumstances, while their successors may be forced to yield some of their control to the lineages. These sorts of shifts in the location of governmental functions may occur a number of times in the history of a society before the political structure is stabilized.

Lineages do not inevitably evolve into centralized states, but there are some conditions which encourage the development of a strong central government. First, the natural growth and dissolution of lineage segments may lead to some segments becoming more populous and therefore more powerful than other segments. In this case the leaders of the strong segments will have more influence than the leaders of weaker segments and may be able to exercise control over their neighbors. Second, individuals who are placed in leadership roles, even temporarily, have a vested interest in maintaining their positions and often have the means to increase their status and power. They may be able to profit from the control of trade or the distribution of property captured in the wars that they have fought. They are therefore able to add to their own wealth and to attract followers who hope to benefit from the leaders' patronage. In the process, lineage ties are weakened and individuals come to depend more heavily on the political elite.

Finally, a society's lineages may simply cease to function effectively as political organizations. The society may become too large or diverse to permit the sort of consensus on which lineage government depends. In this case the lineages may become fragmented and unable to meet the society's economic and political needs. If these needs can be satisfied by established leaders, then the society will be encouraged to desert the lineage system in favor of some sort of centralized state.

THE IMPLICATIONS OF
THE ANTHROPOLOGICAL EVIDENCE
The Formulation of New Hypotheses

When the biblical picture of premonarchical Israel is reexamined in the light of the anthropological data on the structure and functions of lineage systems, there are enough similarities between the two bodies of material to support the general thesis that early Israel was organized as a system of lineages. As in all such systems, the various components of Israelite society were related to each other horizontally and vertically by using the idiom of kinship. The lineages occupied specific geographical areas and occasionally quarreled over lineage boundaries. Although on occasion lineage segments were capable of acting together as a single large lineage, for the most part lineage interaction took place at the lower levels of the social structure. The Israelite lineages had a variety of leaders, although until the rise of the monarchy political power seems to have been reserved to the lineages and was only sporadically and temporarily vested in a centralized government.

The general congruence of the anthropological and biblical evidence suggests that the more detailed comparative material can be useful in elaborating the Old Testament's picture of Israel's early history. However, this sort of historical reconstruction can be done safely only if the biblical and archaeological evidence is allowed to remain the controlling factor in the process. This means that the anthropological evidence can only be used to formulate new hypotheses which can then be tested against the ancient data. The comparative material may suggest new questions to be asked of the biblical text and may help to explain previously obscure details, but in the last analysis a hypothesis can be considered valid only if it is capable of incorporating all of the textual and archaeological evidence. The hypothetical historical reconstruction may say *more* than the ancient sources, but it cannot say *less*.

The Testing of Hypotheses: Israel's Premonarchical Judicial System

As an example of the development and testing of anthropologically derived hypotheses, we may consider the history of Israel's premonarchical judicial system.[14] There is no archaeological evidence on the judiciary, so any historical reconstruction must be based solely on the Old Testament. Only a few texts are relevant to the subject, and the historiographic reliability of some of these has been challenged. The clearest picture of early legal activity comes from Joshua 7, the story of the trial of Achan after his theft of devoted objects from Jericho, and from Judges 19—21, a complex account of the tribes' reaction to the rape of a Levite's concubine. However, both passages bear the clear stamp of the Deuteronomistic Historian, and

14. I have discussed this subject in greater detail in Robert R. Wilson, "Enforcing the Covenant: The Mechanisms of Judicial Authority in Early Israel," in *The Quest for the Kingdom of God: Essays in Honor of George E. Mendenhall*, ed. Herbert B. Huffmon *et. al.*(Winona Lake, Ind.: Eisenbrauns, 1983).

most scholars consider them to be influenced by later Deuteronomic theology. In addition, historians sometimes cite as evidence the narrative of Moses's appointment of judges (Exod. 18:13-27; cf. Deut. 1:9-18), the Deuteronomic laws dealing with judicial proceedings (Deut. 16:18-20; 17:2-13; 19:15-21), and the account of negotiations over Ruth's marriage (Ruth 4), but these too are normally considered to be reflections of relatively late judicial theories and practices that have been retrojected into earlier periods. More likely to be reliable are the Deuteronomic texts which speak of judicial hearings conducted by village elders at the town gate (Deut. 19:1-13; 21:1-9, 18-21; 22:13-21; 25:4-10), although these passages give few details about the proceedings. Finally, most scholars would agree that the stories of Jacob's dealings with Laban (Genesis 31) and Judah's treatment of his daughter-in-law Tamar (Genesis 38) are accurate indications that family heads had virtually absolute judicial authority over those in their households.

This meager data on the judicial system can be supplemented considerably once it is assumed that early Israel was organized as a lineage system. We have already described in some detail the tendency of lineages to generate conflict, and we have examined the processes by which disputes are negotiated in order to maintain lineage unity. On the basis of this knowledge it is possible to formulate a hypothetical reconstruction of Israel's lineage judiciary. Assuming that Israel followed normal patterns, we would suppose that at the lower levels of the social system legal authority was exercised by elders who were able to require that their own kin adhere to commonly accepted social norms. In cases of conflict between larger lineage segments, Israel presumably lacked a centralized judicial authority capable of settling disputes and therefore relied on a process of negotiation. We would expect the effectiveness of this system to have diminished as more people became involved, and in the case of conflicts between large lineages it is likely that satisfactory solutions were very difficult to achieve. As a result, large Israelite lineages were probably unstable and prone to fragment over issues that could not be resolved by negotiation.

When this reconstruction is tested against the Old Testament texts, all of the biblical evidence seems to be accommodated. The references to the judicial activities of the elders are consistent with what we know of the role these leaders play at the lower levels of lineage systems. The strong judicial authority of family heads is to be expected in small lineages, and the Old Testament's lack of references to a central judicial system is also in keeping with the decentralized lineage judiciary. The hierarchical system of central judges mentioned in Exod. 18:13-27 and Deut. 1:9-18 does not fit well into the normal lineage system, so scholars are probably correct in seeing these passages as retrojections of the later monarchical system. Furthermore, the descriptions of judicial procedures in Joshua 7 and Judges 19—21 are good illustrations of the strengths and weaknesses of lineage justice. Both of these texts certainly have a long editorial history and have been shaped to fill the theological needs of the Deuteronomistic Historian. However, they still seem to reflect a knowledge of premonarchical society.

The story of Achan begins with the note that he violated the holy war regulations by taking from Jericho objects devoted to God. Yet because there were no witnesses to the theft, the people do not realize that there is a problem until they are defeated in battle. They inquire of God in order to uncover the reason for the defeat and are told of the crime (Josh. 7:1-12). At the same time, the inquiry specifies a procedure for discovering the guilty party and indicates the penalty which is to be imposed. The people are to gather before God and cast lots to locate the thief, who is then to be burned (Josh. 7:13-15). We have already noted that this method of determining guilt is usually avoided in lineage trials because it removes the opportunity for negotiation. The lots will inevitably identify someone as the culprit, and the decision cannot be appealed. Once guilt has been established, the death penalty must be applied, so there is no room for argument about a fair punishment. In such situations communal dissension is likely to occur, so the lineage elders do everything possible to gather popular support for the verdict. Joshua follows these standard procedures in conducting Achan's trial. When the lots identify Achan as the guilty party, Joshua encourages him to confess his guilt in order to demonstrate the accuracy of the oracles. Achan does so and even furnishes additional proof of his guilt by describing the hiding place of the stolen goods, something that only the real thief would know (Josh. 7:19-21). The goods are recovered by several messengers and shown to the people to indicate the truth of Achan's confession (Josh. 7:22-23). This chain of events convinces the people of Achan's guilt, and they join with Joshua in carrying out the sentence. The stoning of Achan can thus be understood as a communal ritual that reaffirms the unity of the society (Josh. 7:24-26).

While the story of Achan reflects typical judicial proceedings in small lineages, the account of the rape of the Levite's concubine illustrates the difficulties of adjudicating disputes between very large lineages such as the Israelite tribes. According to Judges 19—21, some Benjamites living in Gibeah raped and killed a Levite's concubine, a Judahite woman from Bethlehem. Because the crime involved individuals from two different towns in two different tribes, the matter had to be handled at the tribal level, with the result that very large lineages were involved. Consensus is difficult to achieve at this level of lineage activity, and the weaknesses of the system are graphically illustrated in the remainder of the story. The tribes assemble at Mizpah to decide on a course of action. In the presence of all of the people, the lineage elders hear testimony from the Levite, and the assembly decides to punish the men from Gibeah (Judg. 20:1-11). The Israelites send messages to the Benjamite lineages requesting that they hand over the men from Gibeah, but for some reason, the Benjamites refuse. Negotiations fail, and the Israelites resort to military action in order to enforce the court's verdict. This move destroys the unity of Israel and escalates into a full-scale war. However, the Israelites apparently do not gather full communal support for their plans, for there is considerable indecision in implementing them. The people seek oracular advice before proceeding with the battle (Judg. 20:12-18), but when they are defeated their confidence is shaken, and they become unsure of their course of action. They weep all night and again inquire of God for instructions (Judg. 20:23). This process is repeated yet a third time before the Israelites finally obtain victory (Judg. 20:24-28). However, even after the punishment has been carried out, the people regret the break in the social structure brought about by the ostracism of Benjamin. They therefore devise a plan to reconstitute Benjamin as an Israelite lineage and to restore the unity of the nation (Judg. 21:1-24).

The Search for New Data

Although anthropological evidence can be used to elaborate the biblical data bearing on a particular historical question, this is not the only function of comparative material in the study of Israelite history. The work of anthropologists can be used to suggest a wider range of questions to put to the biblical texts and can aid in the formulation of more detailed hypotheses. However, extrabiblical evidence can also raise questions which the ancient sources cannot answer and can lead to the formulation of hypotheses which cannot currently be tested. In this way comparative material may encourage a search for new data or may force us to see old data in a new way.

An example of this phenomenon may be seen in the anthropological evidence on the growth and dissolution of lineages and the relation of this process to the creation of centralized political systems. Studies of lineage systems suggest the hypothesis that the rise of the Israelite monarchy was possible both because of the increasing power of certain political leaders and because of a weakening of the traditional lineage system. Israelite lineages might have become weaker for a number of reasons, but a likely cause would have been the growing ineffectiveness of the system. Lineages operate most efficiently when they are small, and there seems to be an inherent limit on the number of people that can be incorporated in a functioning lineage. The anthropological evidence on this point is incomplete, but one of the largest known lineages has a depth of fourteen to seventeen generations and includes about 800,000 people, a figure which is probably close to the upper population limit for lineage systems. However, lineages of this size are rare, and normal lineages usually have a depth of three to six generations and unify groups of 200 to 1,300 people.[15]

The population of premonarchical Israel is difficult to estimate. The segmented genealogies that have been preserved rarely exceed a depth of six generations, a fact that might imply the existence of lineages containing no more than 1,500 people. However, the Old Testament's own traditional census figures (Numbers 1; 26) point to a population well in excess of the limit of 800,000 people suggested by the anthropological evidence.[16] Scholars do not agree on the accuracy of these traditional figures, but if they are even close to being correct, then the nation of Israel in the period of the judges had already reached or exceeded the maximum size of a functioning lineage system. If so, then we can suspect that national consensus on any issue was difficult to achieve and that most political, economic, and religious activities took place at or below the tribal level. If in addition, as Gottwald and Mendenhall suggest, the invading Israelite tribes were augmented by the incorporation of foreign populations, then the stage would have been set for the rapid dissolution of the traditional social system. The lineages would have been too large and too diverse to function effectively even at the tribal level and ultimately would have fragmented as they failed to meet the needs of the overall society. If at the same time temporary leaders were able to

---

15. Laura Bohannan, "A Genealogical Charter," *Africa* 22(1952):301.
16. For a discussion of these census figures, see George E. Mendenhall, "The Census Lists of Numbers 1 and 26," *JBL* 77(1958):52–66.

increase their political power because they had strong economic or military support, then a relatively smooth transition from a lineage system to a monarchical system would have become a possibility. At the moment there is little archaeological or biblical evidence to support this hypothesis, but such evidence might be obtained by properly directing future research so as to uncover new data.[17] Archaeological studies of settlement patterns, for example, might throw light on the growth and disintegration of lineages, while surveys of house sites and commercial installations might indicate the growing power of individual leaders. In a similar way the biblical texts themselves might be restudied to resolve the problem of the size of Israel's population and to determine the amount of national unity that actually existed before the monarchy. The Old Testament itself may contain evidence that has not previously been used because its relevance has not been recognized. In this case the comparative anthropological material clearly presses scholars to seek new data that will help to explain why Israel made the transition from lineage system to monarchical state.

THE LIMITS OF
THE ANTHROPOLOGICAL APPROACH

Although up to this point we have stressed the value of using anthropological evidence in the study of Israelite history, it is also important to recognize the limits of this approach. The modern material does not supply a comprehensive sociological description which can then be used to reconstruct ancient Israelite society. To use the contemporary material in this way would be to ignore the real possibility that ancient and modern societies are essentially different in ways not yet fully recognized. In addition, careless use of contemporary evidence may obscure the unique features in the societies being studied. Rather, at most anthropological work can help to elaborate and interpret ancient evidence and may contribute to the coherence of a historical reconstruction. Modern evidence cannot prove the truth or falsity of a reconstruction. That task can be accomplished only by testing the reconstruction against the available ancient data.

---

17. Preliminary work on this subject has already been done by Flanagan, "Chiefs in Israel," pp. 47–73.

IV

Understanding Literary Forms:
An Anthropological Perspective
on the Old Testament
Genealogies

Anthropological research has played a role in the critical study of Old Testament literature since the end of the nineteenth century. In particular, the early form critics, such as Hermann Gunkel, recognized that contemporary folklorists could help the biblical scholar to understand more clearly the way in which living societies create, preserve, and use oral literature in specific social settings.[1] This sort of information was of great value in form-critical studies that were interested in uncovering the original oral form of the present biblical text.

Since the days of Gunkel, folklore studies have become more sophisticated, and scholars now know a great deal about oral literature and the motifs that it contains. Yet, for several reasons this data has not had the dramatic influence on Old Testament interpretation that Gunkel and his followers had originally hoped. In the first place, Gunkel's form-critical program assumed that much of the Old Testament was originally in oral form and that oral literary genres are well enough preserved in the written text to permit their recovery. In the opinion of many modern critics, these assumptions are likely to be true in the case of the early prophetic literature but are more doubtful in later prophecy and in narratives, where the oral origins of the bulk of the literature are difficult to demonstrate. Particularly in the Pentateuch and the Deuteronomistic History (Joshua through Kings), the present written prose narratives seem far removed from the largely poetic oral epics that have been studied by folklorists. Even if it is assumed that a poetic original underlies our written prose text, it is not at all certain that this earlier material can be recovered.

---

1. Hermann Gunkel, "Die Israelitische Literatur," in *Die Kultur der Gegenwart*, ed. Paul Hinneberg (Berlin: B. G. Teubner, 1906), I/7:51–102.

More research needs to be done on the transformations that take place in oral literary genres when they are fixed in writing. Until such information is available, it may not automatically be assumed that a particular literary genre has the same form and function at both the oral and written levels. This uncertainty hampers the form-critical enterprise by casting doubt on the recoverability of oral genres.

Second, Gunkel's form-critical program called for an investigation of the social settings in which Israel's literature originally functioned, and he was a pioneer in using anthropological data to reconstruct aspects of Israelite society. By this means Gunkel hoped to revivify the literature and make it more comprehensible to the modern reader. However, subsequent form critics have experienced some difficulties in elaborating Gunkel's early attempts to sketch the social contexts of Old Testament literature. This is so at least partially because contemporary folklorists have concentrated their research on literary motifs and patterns and have not supplied biblical scholars with adequate information on the way in which oral genres actually function in the everyday lives of the people who use them. Without such comparative material it is unlikely that major advances can be made in understanding the social matrix of Israelite literature.

Finally, Gunkel's form-critical method seems to have assumed the existence of archetypical literary genres that are shared by a number of societies. If such common genres exist, then folklore studies should illuminate the Old Testament by providing a number of detailed literary parallels to the biblical genres. However, subsequent research has shown that Israelite literature has more unique features than Gunkel suspected, and for this reason folklorists have been able to supply very few examples of genres that closely resemble those found in the Bible. The same phenomenon can be observed in the area of comparative folklore itself. When the oral literatures of different societies are compared, a number of similar literary genres can be observed, but these genres are parallel only at a fairly high level of abstraction. For this reason folklorists often present their data so as to illustrate general patterns, and as a result biblical scholars have had difficulty finding detailed cross-cultural parallels that help to interpret the specific literary forms of the Old Testament.

Some of the difficulties experienced by contemporary form critics might be resolved by using the work of social anthropologists to supplement the folklore research that biblical scholars have traditionally used as the source of their comparative material. From the standpoint of form criticism, the value of social anthropological studies is that they usually present their data as part of a comprehensive picture of a particular society. Any literary genres which are discussed are therefore set in their overall social context. Studies of this sort can supply valuable information on the social functions of various types of oral literature and may even shed light on the relationships between oral and written genres. In order to illustrate the potential usefulness of this approach, we will examine a simple literary genre, the genealogy. Oral and written genealogies are found in a number of societies, so there is ample evidence for comparative research. In addition, the biblical examples of the genre have not been clearly understood and are therefore likely candidates for study from a cross-cultural perspective.

THE NATURE OF THE PROBLEM

Throughout much of the history of Old Testament interpretation, the genealogies have been considered to be historical sources that preserve accurate information about the kinship ties between individuals and groups. The genealogies could therefore be used to reconstruct early Israelite history and might even play a role in chronological calculations. This traditional view of the genealogies began to change with the rise of critical biblical scholarship in the nineteenth century, when scholars began to challenge the accuracy of the Bible's genealogical data. Early critical interpreters tended to see the genealogies as late fabrications having little historiographic worth, while more recent scholarship has held that they are artificial creations used as literary links to join together earlier narrative segments.[2]

One of the reasons for contemporary scepticism about the Old Testament genealogies is that the preserved genealogical information is sometimes fluid and contradictory. In parallel genealogies the same individuals or groups are occasionally assigned different kinship connections, a situation that encourages scholars to assume that one genealogy is accurate while the other one is not. Interpreters are therefore likely to try to resolve the contradiction, either by arguing for the textual or historical accuracy of one version over the other or by trying to see literary significance in the differences. If the contradictions cannot be resolved, then scholars may simply ignore

2. For a more complete survey of scholarly research on the Old Testament genealogies, see Robert R. Wilson, "The Old Testament Genealogies in Recent Research," *JBL* 94(1975):169–89.

both genealogies or assume that they have no importance for the interpretation of the text.

THE CHOICE OF AN ANTHROPOLOGICAL APPROACH

Rather than attempt to refine the scholarly techniques for dealing with genealogical contradiction, a more fruitful approach to the problem may be to reexamine the standard perception of the nature of genealogy. This can best be done by studying the way in which oral and written genealogies are actually used in societies having a social structure similar to that of ancient Israel. In the previous chapter we suggested that early Israel was a lineage system that eventually developed into a monarchical state. Research done by social anthropologists indicates that societies organized in both of these ways use genealogies for a wide variety of purposes. Furthermore, because of the social anthropologists' interest in the structure and functioning of society, they have studied the roles that genealogies play in everyday life. This information is useful in understanding the social matrix of the Old Testament genealogies and may also allow us to compare the forms and functions of written and oral genealogies.

A SURVEY OF THE ANTHROPOLOGICAL EVIDENCE

Genealogies are oral or written expressions of the descent of a person or persons from one or more ancestors. As literary genres, genealogies are relatively simple and have only two basic forms. When a genealogy traces more than one line of descent from a single ancestor, then the genealogy is segmented or branched, having the shape of the familiar "family tree." If a genealogy traces only one line of descent from a single ancestor, then the genealogy is linear and exhibits no segmentation. Because a genealogy traces descent, it must state or imply the kinship ties that link the people within it. Whether the genealogy is part of a larger narrative or is a simple list of names, an indication of kinship must be present either inside of the genealogy or outside of it. In the former case kinship terms will appear between the names in the genealogy ("X was the son of Y the son of Z"). In the latter case the operative kinship term will appear before or after a list of names to indicate how they are to be related ("the daughters of X: Y and Z").[3]

---

3. Wilson, *Genealogy and History*, pp. 8–10.

Segmented Genealogies and Lineage Systems

Societies that are organized as lineage systems use segmented genealogies as expressions or mnemonics of the lineage. The genealogies serve as mirrors for the lineage structure and reflect the depth, breadth, and fluidity which are characteristic of lineages. Like the lineages that they represent, oral segmented genealogies have an average maximum depth of twelve generations. However, many tribes cannot recite oral genealogies that are this extensive, and in these cases genealogical depth does not usually exceed five generations.

Lineage genealogies are rarely cited in their full segmented form. In large lineages the average person is incapable of reproducing the entire genealogy, and even knowledgeable specialists do not often have the occasion to cite more than the genealogy of their own segment and that of adjacent segments. For the most part, genealogies are recited for particular purposes, and only immediately relevant information is included. Since public recitations are also the occasions on which lineage members increase their genealogical knowledge, the learning process is often a slow and haphazard one.

In our earlier discussion of lineages we noted that individuals and even whole segments can move to new positions in the lineage structure because of shifts in status, power, or social function. Because segmented genealogies are representations of the lineage, they too must change as the lineage structure changes. Thus, for example, an individual who gains social prestige or political power may move to a higher level in the lineage genealogy. In the same way, when a segment changes its political, social, or economic alliances within the lineage, a corresponding change takes place in the lineage genealogy. Names are added to a genealogy as new lineage members are born and as outsiders are incorporated. Names may disappear through the simple process of forgetting, a process which is accelerated when the names involved are not those of lineage heads and have no structural significance.

Genealogical fluidity may not represent actual changes in the lineage structure but may reflect changes which the reciter of the genealogy wishes to promote. Individuals seeking higher status or pressing a claim to political office may present a revised genealogy in the hope that the society will accept the social reality that the genealogy represents.

Oral segmented genealogies function in several different spheres of social life. In the domestic sphere, genealogies express the kinship relationships that determine everyday conduct, individual rights, and social obligations. Genealogies define permissible marriages and regulate inheritance. In some cases they may also determine the socially acceptable directions of territorial expansion and draw the boundaries outside of which feuds may take place. In the politico-jural sphere, genealogies are used to reflect the structure of governmental power in the lineage and may also play a role in determining who is eligible to fill lineage offices. Tribal groups may cite an appropriate genealogy in order to justify their claim to land, and genealogies may be used to express friendly or hostile relationships between large lineages.

Finally, segmented genealogies may function in the religious sphere if they represent cultic relationships between individuals and groups. Genealogies may serve to define the boundaries of the religious community and indicate the persons who may legitimately participate in the lineage's religious life. Cultic status and authority may also be expressed genealogically, and in lineages where religious offices are inherited, genealogies regulate succession by clarifying the relative claims of the various candidates. Societies having a cult of the dead may use genealogies to record the ancestral names that must be invoked, and in some cases genealogies may actually be recited as part of the ritual.

The configuration of a given lineage may change depending on the social sphere in which it is functioning. Thus, for example, domestic relationships based on genuine kinship may not be the same as political or economic ties. As the lineage's structure changes, the genealogy that reflects that structure must also change in order to be an accurate representation of the lineage. This process may give rise to several apparently contradictory genealogies which are in fact accurate records of the lineage functioning in particular contexts.

The fluidity which is required of effectively functioning lineage genealogies is facilitated when they are preserved and used orally. When genealogies are written down, they are frozen in a single form, and the possibility of genealogical change is diminished, although not eliminated entirely. The problem of conflicting genealogies becomes more acute, and the written record hinders the rational adjustment of genealogies to fit current communal perceptions. Written segmented genealogies are simply not flexible enough to meet the needs of a dynamic lineage system, and for this reason lineage-based societies tend to avoid making written records of their genealogies.

Linear Genealogies

Linear genealogies have only two important formal characteristics: depth and fluidity. Like their segmented counterparts, oral linear genealogies are normally between five and ten generations in depth, although if a society does preserve genealogies that are longer than this, they are more likely to be linear than segmented. Linear genealogies grow naturally as the names of newborn children are added to the lower end of the genealogy, and names may also be added in the middle of the list. Similarly, names may change their internal positions. However, the most common type of fluidity in linear genealogies is the loss of names, a process sometimes called telescoping. This phenomenon almost always appears in the middle of the genealogy rather than at the beginning or end, and its location is not accidental. The names at the lower end of the genealogy are those of living people and are therefore unlikely to change unless interpersonal relationships change or unless the individuals involved migrate or die. In the same way, the individuals at the top of the genealogy are the descendants of the founder of the line. These names are usually firmly fixed in the society's historical or mythological lore and are functionally the most important in the genealogy, so they are not likely to be altered. However, the names in the middle of the list have no functional significance, and it is in this area that fluidity is most likely to occur.

Linear genealogies have essentially only one function. They serve to support an individual's claim to status, power, or property by linking the individual with an early ancestor. This function may be carried out in any social arena. In the domestic sphere, linear genealogies may be cited to justify inheritance rights or to secure hereditary leadership positions. The same is true in the religious sphere and in the politico-jural sphere, where linear genealogies are used by office holders to defend their right to their positions. Genealogies often serve to control access to the priesthood and in some societies help to determine who may fill political positions. The clearest examples of such genealogies are the king lists and royal genealogies maintained in many societies to demonstrate the continuity and legitimacy of the monarchy. No matter what the actual historical facts may be, each reigning monarch is seen as the son and legal heir of his predecessor. The current ruler traces his ancestry to the first person to exercise kingship and in this way genealogically defends his position against any existing rivals. When a challenger does arise, he too must produce a genealogy in order to demonstrate that his claim to power is more valid than that of the incumbent. In this way a number of conflicting genealogies may spring up, each one seeking to certify its user's right to rule. Disputes of this sort are also likely to occur when the throne becomes vacant. In hereditary monarchies genealogies are often among the weapons used in struggles over the succession.

In contrast to segmented genealogies, linear genealogies have the same function at both the oral and written levels. They do not need to change constantly in order to mirror structural changes in the lineage, so their value is not limited when they are frozen in writing. In fact writing may enhance the effectiveness of linear genealogies by making it possible for an individual to recall a larger number of names and thus reproduce a more impressive and persuasive genealogy.[4]

THE IMPLICATIONS OF
THE ANTHROPOLOGICAL EVIDENCE
The Formulation of New Hypotheses

The anthropological evidence indicates that a genealogy's structure is closely related to its social function. When the function changes, the structure must also change if the genealogy is not to lose its effectiveness. This is particularly true in the case of segmented genealogies, which must be flexible enough to reflect alterations in the shape of the lineage. When such genealogies are prevented from changing by being fixed in writing, they simply become historical examples of lineage configurations that no longer exist. The society then creates new genealogies to mirror the new lineage structures, even though these genealogies conflict with the ones preserved in writing. However, the people using the genealogies are not disturbed by the conflict, for they are aware of the proper interpretation of each genealogy. An exception to the rule that genealogical fluidity has functional significance occurs in the case of linear genealogies, where names in the middle of the list have no function and are therefore likely to appear in a variable order or even to disappear entirely.

The close links between genealogical form, content, and function

---

4. I have discussed the anthropological evidence more thoroughly in Wilson, *Genealogy and History*, pp. 18–55, where a full bibliography of anthropological sources may be found. Note in particular Iona Mayer, "From Kinship to Common Descent: Four-Generation Genealogies among the Gusii," *Africa* 35(1965):366–84; Emrys Peters, "The Proliferation of Segments in the Lineage of the Bedouin of Cyrenaica," *JRAI* 90(1960):29–53; Ian Cunnison, *Baggara Arabs* (Oxford: At the Clarendon Press, 1966), pp. 144–49, 187–90, 213–18; Jack Goody, ed., *Succession to High Office* (New York and Cambridge: Cambridge University Press, 1966); and L. Bohannan, "A Genealogical Charter," 301–15.

suggest that scholars can no longer be content simply to point out discrepancies in the Old Testament genealogies but must seek to determine whether or not apparent contradictions have functional significance. The functional question must be asked not only at the oral level but also at the literary level, for one would expect a society knowledgeable in the idiom of genealogy to incorporate that knowledge in its literature. The wisdom of asking a broader range of questions can be tested by examining briefly two Old Testament genealogies containing apparent contradictions.

The Testing of the Hypotheses

The Descendants of Adam

In Gen. 4:1-2 the Yahwist begins the story of the first murder with a description of the birth of Adam's two sons: Cain and Abel. After giving an account of the killing and of Cain's subsequent punishment, the narrator traces Cain's genealogy through his son Enoch to Lamech. The genealogy is linear and lists Cain's descendants as Enoch, Irad, Mahujael, Methushael, and finally Lamech. With Lamech the genealogy becomes segmented, and the text presents information on the daughter and three sons of Lamech, including notes on their occupations and their role as cultural innovators. Following the tracing of the genealogy of Cain, the writer returns to the story of Adam and records the birth of his third son, Seth.

A very different account of Adam's descendants is given in Genesis 5 by the Priestly Writer. Here the author retells the story of the first humans, partially paraphrasing and partially quoting the priestly creation account in Gen. 1:27-28: "When God created man, he made him in the likeness of God. Male and female he created them, and he blessed them . . . " (Gen. 5:1-2). The writer then uses a linear genealogy to trace Adam's descendants through a line of firstborn sons from Seth through Lamech to Noah. The following names are listed: Adam, Seth, Enosh, Kenan, Mahalalel, Jared, Enoch, Methuselah, Lamech, and Noah.

Scholars have long noted that these two genealogies are near duplicates of each other and that they contain contradictions which are difficult to reconcile. In Genesis 4 Cain is clearly portrayed as the firstborn son of Adam, while Seth is unambiguously Adam's third son (Gen. 4:1, 25). In contrast Gen. 5:3 implies that Seth is Adam's firstborn, and there is no mention of Cain or Abel. Both Gen. 4:26 and Gen. 5:6 agree that Enosh was the son of Seth, but Genesis 5 also makes him the ancestor of a line that Gen. 4:17-18 connects with Cain. In Gen. 4:19-22 Lamech is given three sons—Jabal, Jubal, and Tubal-cain—and one daughter, Naamah, while Gen. 5:28-29 mentions only Lamech's firstborn son, Noah, who is not mentioned at all in Genesis 4. Finally, the names which are duplicated in the two genealogies do not always appear in the same order.

Interpreters have attempted to deal with these contradictions by proposing a harmonization, by emending the text, and by simply attributing them to an editor lacking literary sensitivity, but a different approach is suggested by the anthropological data on the functions of genealogies. The extrabiblical evidence indicates that the structure of a genealogy may change when its function changes, and this observation prompts the hypothesis that the genealogical fluidity in Genesis 4 and 5 may have functional significance. In fact a closer examination of the two passages indicates that this may well be the case.

In Gen. 4:17-26 the interest of the Yahwist seems to be in describing the origins of various aspects of civilization. Either Cain or his son Enoch is credited with building the first city, while Lamech is the first practitioner of blood vengeance. Lamech's sons are the ancestors of all tent-dwellers, cattle-keepers, musicians, and smiths, while Seth's son Enosh is apparently the first to worship God. However, by including all of these figures in the same genealogy as ancestors of the first murderer, Cain, the Yahwist has given a negative cast to the origins of civilized life. These early humans inherited from their ancestor a tendency toward violence, a fact demonstrated by the song of vengeance sung by Cain's descendant, Lamech (Gen. 4:23-24). For the Yahwist, then, the whole of Genesis 4 illustrates the spread of evil and violence that become the central concern of the flood story.

In contrast with this negative view, the Priestly Writer has a more positive opinion of human beings. To counterbalance the Yahwist's work, the Priestly Writer emphasizes that humans were created in the divine image and blessed on the day of creation. In Genesis 5 the narrator traces the transmission of the image and the blessing through a succession of firstborn sons, so that Noah's righteousness (Gen. 6:9) is portrayed as inherited from Adam, the original recipient of the blessing. Because the Priestly Writer stressed the blessing, it was not possible to include the murderer Cain in the genealogy, so the ancestral line had to begin with the only other living son of Adam mentioned in the text, Seth. The Yahwist's genealogy was then used to construct a linear genealogy connecting Adam and Noah, but genealogical fluidity was encouraged by the fact that, as is typical of linear genealogies, the names in the middle of the list had no functional significance. The apparent contradictions between Genesis 4 and 5 thus become comprehensible when the differing functions of the two genealogies are recognized.[5]

The Descendants of Abraham

Although the Old Testament is normally interested only in those descendants of Abraham that become the eponymous ancestors of Israel, the text does record other branches of his family. One of these texts, the genealogy of Abraham's children by Keturah, contains some striking genealogical contradictions that have long puzzled scholars. In Gen. 25:1-6 the Yahwist records a segmented genealogy that relates four generations of descendants. The whole genealogy need not concern us here, but one segment is of particular interest. According to this text, Abraham had six sons by Keturah, and one of these, Jokshan, had two sons, Sheba and Dedan. The latter two names are well attested as tribal names in extrabiblical sources and are usually taken to be inhabitants of the Arabian Peninsula. By portraying them as grandsons, the genealogy relates them fairly closely to Abraham and indeed places them on the same genealogical level as Jacob/Israel.[6]

However, this picture differs sharply from the one recorded in the so-called table of nations in Genesis 10.[7] This complex text is usually thought to be the combined work of the Yahwist and Priestly Writer, but if the traditional scholarly analysis of the chapter is accurate, it preserves two different accounts of the genealogies of Sheba and Dedan, both of which conflict with Gen. 25:1-6. In the Yahwist's portion of the table of nations, Dedan does not appear, but Sheba is made one of the descendants of Shem, that son of Noah who is the eponymous ancestor of all of the Semites, including Israel. According to this genealogy, Eber had two sons, Peleg and Joktan (= Jokshan?). In Gen. 11:16-26 a six-generation linear genealogy is traced from Peleg to Abraham, while the Yahwist in Gen. 10:26 assigns Peleg's brother Joktan thirteen sons, among whom is Sheba. Sheba is thus in

5. I have discussed this example in greater detail in Wilson, *Genealogy and History*, pp. 138-66.

6. For a discussion of this genealogy in the context of the other Arabian genealogies in the Old Testament, see Fred V. Winnett, "The Arabian Genealogies in the Book of Genesis," in *Translating and Understanding the Old Testament*, ed. Harry Thomas Frank and William L. Reed (Nashville: Abingdon Press, 1970), pp. 171-96.

7. For a discussion of the composition of Genesis 10, see Claus Westermann, *Genesis* (Neukirchen-Vluyn: Neukirchener Verlag, 1974), pp. 662-706.

an earlier generation than is the case in Gen. 25:1–6 and is much more distantly related to Jacob/Israel.

In contrast to the Yahwist, the Priestly Writer makes both Sheba and Dedan sons of Raamah, a grandson of Ham, that son of Noah who is the eponymous ancestor of the Egyptian, African, and Canaanite peoples (Gen. 10:6–7). In this version of the genealogy Sheba and Dedan are even more distantly related to Jacob/Israel than is the case in Gen. 10:21–31 and in fact cannot even be considered to be in the same family of nations.

There is no convincing way to resolve these genealogical conflicts, but they can perhaps be better understood by seeing them against the background of the anthropological evidence. It is doubtful that Israel even knew of lineages sufficiently large to incorporate all of the peoples mentioned in Genesis 10, but the biblical writers may well have used the idiom of genealogy to speak of their relationship with other nations. If so, then it is clear that the three versions of the genealogies of Sheba and Dedan represent three differing perceptions of the closeness of these groups to Israel. There are two ways of explaining these differences. First, they may come from differing historical periods. If so, then the Yahwist's version of the genealogy in Gen. 25:1–6 presumably comes from an early period when relationships were fairly close, while Gen. 10:21–31 and Gen. 10:6–7 must represent later periods, when the relationship grew more distant. Second, it may be that all three of the genealogies are roughly contemporary but represent lineage relationships in different social spheres. Gen. 25:1–6, for example, might represent lineage relationships in geographical terms, while the other genealogies might reflect political or religious relationships. However, with the present biblical evidence there is no way to develop this possibility in greater detail. The most that can be said is that the three versions of the genealogy resemble standard lineage genealogies and have no apparent literary role in the present Old Testament text.

THE LIMITS OF
THE ANTHROPOLOGICAL APPROACH

Although the anthropological material on the forms and functions of genealogies may throw some light on the way in which the Bible uses this literary genre, it is important to notice what this comparative evidence does *not* do for the biblical interpreter. First, the comparative material does not solve the problem of the historiographic worth of the Old Testament genealogies. The anthropological sources indicate that genealogies are records of *perceived* realities, but the value of this sort of evidence for the historian needs to be determined on other grounds. Second, the comparative material suggests that genealogical fluidity may have functional significance, but anthropologists cannot indicate to the biblical scholar which functions are involved in any given case. The extrabiblical data thus provoke the Old Testament interpreter to ask a wider range of questions, but those questions must be answered solely on the basis of the biblical text.

V

Interpreting Israel's Religion: An Anthropological Perspective on the Problem of False Prophecy

The use of anthropology in the critical study of Israel's religion began with the seminal work of Julius Wellhausen and W. Robertson Smith, who attempted to apply contemporary ethnographic research to the problem of reconstructing Israelite religious history. Their work was highly influential and inspired others to follow their lead, but enthusiasm for this type of comparative study waned once scholars began to recognize the methodological problems involved in setting biblical data within a theoretical social-scientific framework.[1] Since the early part of this century, scholars have usually been reluctant to use anthropological studies to interpret features of Israelite religion, although they have been much more willing to use ancient Near Eastern evidence for this purpose.

Even though methodological considerations have certainly been a major cause of this reluctance, theological factors have also been involved. Scholars who have held that Israel's faith was in some way unique have usually argued that extrabiblical evidence is irrelevant to the study of Israelite religion because religious phenomena in other cultures are not truly comparable to those in Israel. If these scholars engage in comparative studies at all, they are usually interested in using cross-cultural data to highlight Israel's uniqueness.[2] To be sure, there is a sense in which every society's religion is unique, for it is shaped by a distinctive history and a particular set of cultural forces. However, once this uniqueness has been recognized, the fact remains that the same general religious phenomena appear in a number of different societies. Even more important, these phenomena tend to

---

1. Hahn, *Old Testament in Modern Research*, pp. 44–82.
2. A prime example of this approach can be seen in the brilliant work of Yehezkel Kaufmann (*The Religion of Israel*, trans. Moshe Greenberg [London: George Allen & Unwin, 1961]), who argued that those features of Israelite religion that had parallels in the ancient Near East were actually part of the popular folk religion and not the official religion of the nation.

play similar social roles in their respective cultures. For this reason comparative anthropological studies can help us to understand more clearly the interaction between religion and society in a particular culture, such as ancient Israel, without requiring that we ignore the religion's distinctive features.

One area in which the usefulness of anthropological research can be demonstrated is the study of Israelite prophecy. Israel's prophets were certainly unique individuals, and in fact they are the paradigms used to identify prophets in other cultures. However, the very existence of prophecy outside of Israel suggests that comparative studies might help us to explore the relationship between prophecy and society in the world of the biblical writers.[3] A more comprehensive knowledge of the nature of this relationship is essential if we are to understand the complexities of Israelite prophecy. This is particularly true in the case of one long-standing problem in prophetic research, the problem of false prophecy.

THE NATURE OF THE PROBLEM
False Prophecy in the Old Testament

The possibility of false prophecy is inherent in any society that tolerates the existence of prophets. This is so because prophecy is essentially a process by which an intermediary (the prophet) facilitates communication between the human and divine realms. In various ways the prophet receives divine messages and then delivers them to human recipients. However, the prophetic experience is basically a private one, even though the prophet may describe it publicly. In the end the prophet's audience can never be sure that the experience took place as described or that the prophet is accurately reporting the divine message. Therefore, the reliability of any prophecy can be questioned, and the threat of false prophecy is always present.

Ancient Israel was fully aware of the difficulties involved in assessing the truth of prophetic claims, and the Old Testament records several suggestions for dealing with the problem, none of them completely satisfactory. In Deut. 18:22 Moses tells the Israelites that a false prophecy can be recognized when it does not come true. By implication, then, true prophecies are those that do come to pass, but unfortunately this test can only be applied retrospectively, long after the time for public decision about the truth claim has passed.

---

3. For an example of such an exploration, see Wilson, *Prophecy and Society.*

Deut. 13:1-5 proposes a limited but more certain test by considering false any prophet who exhorts the people to worship other gods. This test is useful as far as it goes, but it is not applicable to many prophetic oracles. According to Jer. 28:8-9, Jeremiah himself suggested that prophets delivering disaster oracles are more likely to be true prophets than those prophesying peace. This suggestion was presumably based on an observation of past examples of prophecy and fulfillment, but it remains a calculation of probabilities. It is still possible that prophecies of peace might turn out to be accurate, a possibility that Jeremiah himself would surely have supported when he began delivering salvation oracles (Jeremiah 30—32). Finally, the Greek translators of the Old Testament at least partially solved the problem by giving some prophets the title "pseudoprophet" (Jer. 6:13; 26:7, 8, 11, 16; 27:9; 28:1; 29:1, 8; Zech. 13:2), but this characterization is based on interpretations by the translators of the Septuagint and is not present in the Hebrew text.

The prophets were also aware of their credibility problem and devised various means to solve it. Occasionally they offered the people miraculous signs which occurred immediately to demonstrate the truth of prophecies to be fulfilled in the distant future (1 Kgs. 13:3, 5). Some prophets also provided detailed accounts of their initial calls (Isaiah 6; Jeremiah 1; Ezekiel 1) and described their encounters with the divine world (1 Kgs. 22:17-23) in an attempt to support the truth of their oracles.[4] However, such efforts were not always convincing, and in the end the people received little help in adjudicating prophetic claims.

Scholarly Views on False Prophecy

Given the uncertainties that pervade the Old Testament's attempts to deal with false prophecy, it is not surprising that biblical scholars have discussed the issue at great length.[5] A number of different solutions to the problem have been proposed, but at the risk of

4. The notion that the prophets cited their call visions in order to strengthen their authority has recently been challenged by Long, "Prophetic Authority as Social Reality," in *Canon and Authority*, pp. 3-20.

5. For an assessment of the scholarly discussion up to 1971, see James L. Crenshaw, *Prophetic Conflict* (Berlin: Walter de Gruyter, 1971), pp. 13-22. For additional treatments see Martin Buber, "False Prophets," in *On the Bible: Eighteen Studies by Martin Buber*, ed. Nahum M. Glatzer (New York: Schocken Books, 1968), pp. 166-71; Thomas W. Overholt, *The Threat of Falsehood* (Naperville, Ill.: Alec R. Allenson, 1970); Ivo Meyer, *Jeremia und die falschen Propheten* (Freiburg: Universitätsverlag, 1977); Gerhard Münderlein, *Kriterien wahrer und falscher Prophetie* (Bern: Peter Lang, 1979); Frank Lothar Hossfeld and Ivo Meyer, *Prophet gegen Prophet* (Fribourg: Verlag Schweizerisches Katholisches Bibelwerk, 1973); James A. Sanders, "Hermeneutics in True and False Prophecy," in *Canon and Authority*, pp. 21-41; and Simon John DeVries, *Prophet Against Prophet* (Grand Rapids: William B. Eerdmans, 1978).

oversimplification we may arrange them in seven categories. First, some scholars have argued that true prophets could be distinguished from false ones on the basis of the content of their message. False prophets delivered messages of well-being and used a distinctive vocabulary, while true ones did not.[6] Second, attempts have been made to show that false prophets had revelations of lesser quality than those of the true prophets. The true prophets received their oracles through a divine word rather than through a spirit. They were closer to God and stood in the divine council.[7] Third, all cultic prophets are sometimes considered to have been false.[8] Fourth, interpreters have held that true prophets were those best able to correlate their historical and theological traditions with a perceptive reading of their current situation. In this way they knew which oracles were needed at a particular historical moment, a knowledge that the false prophets did not possess.[9] Fifth, a growing number of scholars hold that all Israelite prophets faced pressures toward falsehood. From the outside, the king, the people, and the theological tradition all tried to influence the prophet's oracles, while from the inside, the prophet's own desire for acceptance pressed him to conform to popular expectations. Only those prophets able to resist these influences were able to keep from becoming false prophets.[10] Sixth, it has been argued that false prophets could not be identified by normal people but could be recognized only by a true prophet.[11] Finally, some interpreters hold that so many factors were involved in recognizing false prophets that it is not possible to generalize about the matter.[12]

Each of these tests for false prophecy can claim some support from the Old Testament text, although some approaches are more subjective and therefore less useful than others. However, some solutions cannot accommodate all of the biblical evidence, and it is

6. Gerhard von Rad, "Die falschen Propheten," *ZAW* 51(1933):109-20; A. S. van der Woude, "Micah in Dispute with the Pseudo-Prophets," *VT* 19(1969):244-60.

7. Sigmund Mowinckel, "The 'Spirit' and the 'Word' in the Pre-Exilic Reforming Prophets," *JBL* 53 (1934):199-227; Hans-Joachim Kraus, *Prophetie in der Krisis* (Neukirchen-Vluyn: Neukirchener Verlag, 1964).

8. G. von Rad, "Die falschen Propheten," pp. 109-20.

9. Buber, "False Prophets," pp. 166-71; Sanders, "Hermeneutics," pp. 21-41; Thomas W. Overholt, "Jeremiah 27-29: The Question of False Prophecy," *JAAR* 35(1967):241-49.

10. E. Jacob, "Quelques remarques sur les faux prophètes," *TZ* 13(1957):479-86; Crenshaw, *Prophetic Conflict*, pp. 23-111.

11. Gottfried Quell, *Wahre und falsche Propheten* (Gütersloh: C. Bertelsmann Verlag, 1952).

12. Hossfeld and Meyer, *Prophet gegen Prophet*, pp. 160-62; Eva Osswald, *Falsche Prophetie im Alten Testament* (Tübingen: J. C. B. Mohr, 1962).

likely that the problem is even more complex than even the most perceptive interpreters have realized.

THE CHOICE OF
AN ANTHROPOLOGICAL APPROACH

Given the difficulty of the false prophecy question, it is unlikely that any sort of comparative approach can provide a definitive solution to the problem. However, it is clear that the false prophecy issue has a sociological dimension that has not yet been fully addressed. The prophetic process involves an exchange between prophet and society, and it is within this exchange that decisions about the prophet's authenticity are made. This suggests that the problem might be clarified by examining anthropological research on the various ways that prophets interact with their societies. Because we are interested here in the way the prophet relates to all aspects of his society, the material collected by social anthropologists will again be useful.[13]

A SURVEY OF
THE ANTHROPOLOGICAL EVIDENCE

The Prophet as Intermediary

The prophet stands between the human and divine worlds and has strong ties to both. As a human being delivering divine messages to a specific audience, the prophet is intimately involved with a particular historical society. Yet at the same time the prophet participates in the supernatural world, which is the source of his oracles. Although both aspects of the prophet's existence must be carefully studied in order to obtain an accurate understanding of the prophetic process, scholars have often concentrated on the second.

In contemporary scholarship the prophet's relationship to the supernatural world is frequently explained in psychological or

---

13. I have discussed this material in detail in Wilson, *Prophecy and Society*, pp. 21–88, where extensive bibliographical references may be found. The following are particularly important: John Beattie and John Middleton, ed., *Spirit Mediumship and Society in Africa* (New York: Africana Publishing Corporation, 1969); Jane Belo, *Trance in Bali* (New York: Columbia University Press, 1960); E. Bourguignon, "The Self, the Behavioral Environment, and the Theory of Spirit Possession," in *Context and Meaning in Cultural Anthropology*, ed. M. E. Spiro (New York: Free Press, 1965), pp. 39–60; Dorothy Emmet, "Prophets and Their Societies," *JRAI* 86(1956):13–23; Peter Fry, *Spirits of Protest* (New York and Cambridge: Cambridge University Press, 1976); I. M. Lewis, *Ecstatic Religion* (Baltimore: Penguin Books, 1971); Middleton, *Lugbara Religion*; John Middleton and E. H. Winter, ed., *Witchcraft and Sorcery in East Africa* (London: Routledge and Kegan Paul, 1963); R. Prince, ed., *Trance and Possession States* (Montreal: R. M. Bucke Memorial Society, 1968); S. M. Shirokogoroff, *Psychomental Complex of the Tungus* (London: Kegan Paul, Trench, Trubner, 1935); and S. S. Walker, *Ceremonial Spirit Possession in Africa and Afro-America* (Leiden: E. J. Brill, 1972).

sociological terms. Thus, for example, psychologists tend to see in prophetic behavior the symptoms of trance, a psychological and physiological state marked by a loss of control over bodily and mental processes and accompanied by altered views of reality and extreme sensitivity to outside stimuli. In extreme cases the individual loses touch with reality entirely and must be considered mentally ill. In the opinion of many researchers, certain individuals are psychologically or sociologically predisposed to become prophets. The sensitive person has a mystical experience that leads to becoming a prophet. The "charismatic" individual becomes a prophet by receiving a "call" which validates his claim to special status and authority. The psychotic or neurotic goes into a trance and is accredited as a prophet. The social misfit consciously exhibits prophetic behavior in order to enhance his social status.

The difficulty with this sort of approach is that it cannot easily be applied to all prophets. Some prophets display no symptoms of trance, and not all of them fit the paradigm of the neurotic or charismatic individual. Furthermore, the standard scholarly approach cannot explain why people with the necessary psychological characteristics do not become prophets. Mystics, charismatics, neurotics, and social misfits do not inevitably resort to delivering prophetic oracles.

A more fruitful way of exploring the relationship of the prophet to the supernatural is to look at the way the prophets and their societies describe the process. These descriptions fall into two general categories. First, many societies attribute the characteristic behavior of prophets to some form of spirit possession. During this process, a spirit from the divine realm temporarily takes up residence in the host's body. The host "clothes" or "embodies" the spirit, so that the spirit rather than the individual controls speech and action. In cases where a possessing spirit has distinctive behavioral characteristics, these will be visible in the host and permit onlookers to identify the spirit. Second, divine-human communication may take place when a prophet's soul leaves his body and travels to the divine world. There it has supernatural visions that become the basis for oracles after the prophet's experience is completed.

Prophets and Their Societies

Not all societies react to prophetic claims in the same way, and even within a single society varying evaluations may be made in different cases. In some instances possession and soul migration are viewed negatively. This occurs when the society does not believe in the possibility of divine-human communication or when the characteristic behavior of the prophet is considered to be socially harmful. In either case the would-be prophet is likely to be considered mentally ill or possessed by an evil or demonic spirit. The individual must then be cured or, if that is not possible, must be removed from the society through exile or execution.

Some societies view the prophetic experience negatively but believe that prophetic behavior can be regularized after an initially unwanted case of possession. In this instance, prophets are tolerated so long as their words and actions remain within the expected patterns. If these patterns are broken, then the individual is likely to be restrained and prevented from prophesying.

Finally, certain societies see the prophetic process positively, particularly when the prophet's behavior is completely controlled. In such societies prophecy is likely to play a role in the religious establishment and to have crucial social functions. Because of the importance assigned to prophecy, attempts will often be made to induce a prophetic experience, through the use of artificial stimulation if necessary. However, such techniques are not believed to affect the validity of the prophet's revelation.

In societies where prophecy is tolerated or encouraged, a prophet requires social support throughout the entire prophetic experience. If such support is lacking, the prophet will not be taken seriously and will therefore be ineffective. The process of validation begins when the prophet first claims to have a divine revelation. At this point the society must decide whether or not the prophet's experience is genuine. If the decision is favorable, then the society will tolerate the prophet or even encourage him by integrating him into the religious establishment. However, if the prophet is to continue to be effective, he must have social support throughout his career. In a sense, then, every new prophetic experience must be evaluated and validated by the society. If for some reason the society decides that the prophet's oracles are no longer genuine, it may refuse to see him as a true prophet.

The mechanisms by which societies adjudicate prophetic claims are imperfectly understood and require more extensive study. However, an important factor in the process is the role played by social expectations. Every society has certain commonly held opinions about the nature of the prophetic experience and about typical forms of prophetic behavior. All prophets must conform to these social expectations if they are to be considered true prophets. To put the matter bluntly, societies recognize individuals as true prophets because their words and deeds fit stereotypical patterns of prophetic behavior.

The way in which societies accredit prophets puts a great deal of pressure on would-be prophets to conform to social expectations. The prophets are thus faced with a dilemma. On the one hand they must be true to the divine revelation which they have received. On the other hand they must conform to a social paradigm in order to gain a hearing for their message. Both sides of the equation must be held in a delicate balance if the prophet is to be successful. Prophets usually strike this balance by subconsciously making their speech and actions conform to expected patterns while at the same time insuring that the content of their oracles is consistent with their divine revelation. However, difficulties arise when the balance cannot be maintained because social demands conflict with the prophet's supernatural imperative. Then the prophet must decide whether to deliver the message as he understands it and risk losing necessary social support or to conform to what is expected at the risk of distorting his revelation. This problem becomes even more complex when the society contains groups having different ideas about stereotypical prophetic behavior. In this case the prophet is in the position of deciding which group's expectations to follow. The prophet cannot be accredited by the whole society, and if other groups have their own prophets, then prophetic conflict becomes inevitable.

The Social Location of Prophets

Prophets may function at any level of the social structure and may be found in connection with any group in the society. However, a useful way of talking about the social standing of a given prophet is to locate the individual in relation to the center of the society's social, religious, and political power structure. Those prophets who carry out their activities close to the centers of power may be called *central prophets*. They are likely to play regular roles in the religious establishment and to enjoy a certain amount of social prestige and political power by virtue of their important religious functions. At the other extreme, prophets may be far removed from the power centers and may operate on the fringes of the society. Such *peripheral prophets* have almost no authority within the society as a whole and are usually dispossessed individuals having little status or political power. Prophets, of course, are not confined to the two ends of this spectrum but may appear at any point on the continuum between a society's center and its periphery. It is possible for a society at any given time to contain prophets located at various places on this continuum, and over time a prophet may move from one social location to another. Such conditions can also breed prophetic conflict.

It is important to note that placing a prophet on a social continuum is a relative matter. From the standpoint of a society's religious and political elite, prophets on the fringes of the society are indeed peripheral. They are to be tolerated but can usually be ignored because they are considered to have no political or religious power. However, from the standpoint of a peripheral group supporting a prophet, that prophet is of central importance, for he represents a means by which the group may speak to the whole society. Judgments about centrality or peripherality are therefore seldom made objectively but depend largely on the social location of the people making the judgments.

The Social Functions of Prophecy

Prophecy can have a variety of different social functions, but in general a given prophet's functions are determined by his social location. Peripheral prophecy sometimes enables individuals of low status to improve their personal situations and to obtain a hearing for their message that would not otherwise be possible. While a society might normally ignore such individuals, when they speak with the voices of the spirits they are likely to be accorded a hearing if the audience accepts the spirits' authority.

Peripheral prophets are usually interested in bringing about fairly rapid social change. As representatives of individuals who have been denied access to the society's centers of power, peripheral prophets are concerned to alter fundamental social institutions in order to end social repression and improve the situation of their support group. The social reforms sought by peripheral prophets sometimes involve a reaffirmation of traditional social values and a return to older religious practices and deities. However, the prophets are more likely to demand radical innovations aimed at restructuring the whole society.

In contrast to peripheral prophecy, central prophecy tends to be concerned with the orderly functioning of the social system. If central prophets are official members of the cultic establishment, then they are responsible for providing access to the divine world whenever necessary. They also serve as the representatives of the spirits in affairs of state. As leaders of the society, they must supply supernatural legitimation for the existing social order and provide divine sanctions for traditional religious, political, and social views. This means that central prophets tend to be more conservative than their peripheral counterparts and are likely to oppose unnecessary innovation that might lead to social instability. However, central prophets are by no means totally opposed to social change. Rather they are concerned to regulate the speed at which change takes place. They are interested in promoting gradual and orderly change that will allow the society to maintain its traditions and preserve its stability.

Witchcraft and False Prophecy Accusations

We have seen that prophecy can be a means by which peripheral individuals seek to bring about radical changes in the social structure. Although they are rarely totally successful in this effort, their work is usually at least partially rewarded. Peripheral prophecy thus indirectly helps to maintain social stability by providing an outlet for repressed individuals to express their frustrations. However, there are limits to the amount of prophetic pressure that a society will tolerate. When the demands of peripheral prophets become too radical, they are likely to antagonize the society and invite retaliation.

Societies have several means of restraining prophetic excesses and preventing undue social friction. One of the most important is the witchcraft accusation. In most cultures witches are viewed as malevolent individuals whose aim is to destroy all forms of human and social life. So clever are these figures that they cannot be observed pursuing their evil plans, and only the final results of their work can be seen. Most societies therefore require the death penalty for witchcraft, for only in this way can the witch's power finally be curbed. When a society accuses a prophet of witchcraft, the initial judgment which the society made on the prophet is in effect reversed. Rather than attributing the prophet's behavior to benign spirit contact, the society accuses him of involvement with demonic powers. The witchcraft accusation thus goes beyond a false prophecy accusation, which simply discredits the prophet by denying a divine source for his oracles. When witchcraft accusations are made, the society is able to remove an offending prophet physically, either by killing or banishing him. This move inevitably leads to a rupture in the social structure, for by destroying the prophet the society also rejects the prophet's support group. Most societies are not willing to go this far and instead use the *threat* of a witchcraft accusation as an effective weapon against the excesses of peripheral individuals and groups.

However, the witchcraft accusation is a two-edged sword, for it can also be used by peripheral prophets against vulnerable individuals in the central social structure. Political leaders, priests, and other prophets are likely targets for such accusations, for these figures are prominent exponents of the views that the peripheral prophet seeks to change. By using this technique the prophet not only claims supernatural support for his own views but demolishes his adversary's views by tracing them to demonic origins.

THE IMPLICATIONS OF
THE ANTHROPOLOGICAL EVIDENCE

The Formulation of New Hypotheses:
The Social Roots of Prophetic Conflict

The anthropological evidence suggests that prophetic conflict may be due to a number of factors, among which social forces play a prominent role. If this is so, then we may suspect that debates about false prophecy in Israel also had sociological components and were not simply disputes over theological issues. It is thus reasonable to assume that decisions about true and false prophecy were essentially made by applying sociological criteria to determine which prophetic claims were valid and which were not. Israel presumably went about this process by employing tests similar to those that are used in modern societies. True prophets were those whose words and actions fit the stereotypical behavior of true prophets. However, because of the complexity of Israelite society, we may also assume that various groups in Israel had different notions of how prophets should act and talk. In this case there would have been no general agreement on which prophets were true and which were false, and this lack of agreement would inevitably have led to prophetic conflict. This hypothesis can be tested in a preliminary way by examining the passages in Jeremiah that deal with prophetic disputes.

The Testing of the Hypotheses:
Jeremiah and the False Prophets

Prophetic disputes play an important role in Jeremiah and are the subject of several narratives (Jeremiah 27—29) and collections of oracles (Jer. 5:12-13, 30-31; 6:13-14; 8:10-11; 14:13-16; 23:9-40). However, the narratives in particular have been difficult to interpret,

77

for they seem to provide no firm grounds for distinguishing the true prophet from the false one. For example, in the account of Jeremiah's confrontation with Hananiah (Jeremiah 27—28), both prophets use the same basic speech forms for their oracles and employ similar symbolic actions. To be sure they deliver different messages. Jeremiah advocates surrender to the Babylonians (Jer. 27:1-13), while Hananiah predicts that Jerusalem will be divinely protected from the Babylonian threat and that the previously deported exiles will soon be allowed to return. However, ancient Israelite theological traditions lie behind both of these views. Jeremiah's message consistently follows the views of the Deuteronomistic theology, which held that the election of Jerusalem and the Davidic royal house was contingent on obedience to divine law as understood by the Deuteronomists. As proof for this position Jeremiah could cite accounts of the fall of Shiloh and Samaria, both of which were destroyed as punishment for not obeying the law (Jeremiah 7; 2 Kings 17). On the other hand, Hananiah's message followed the Jerusalemite royal theology, which stressed the unconditional character of the election of the city and its dynasty and God's promise to dwell forever in Jerusalem (2 Samuel 7; Psalm 132). As proof for this position, Hananiah could cite the miraculous deliverance of Jerusalem at the time of Sennacherib's invasion, when Israel's acknowledged sins did not result in the destruction of the city or the removal of the king (2 Kings 18—19; Isaiah 10, 28—31, 33).

Given the lack of obvious distinctions between these two prophets, it is likely that the roots of the conflict lie in the fact that they are representatives of different groups, neither of which accepts the authority of the other's prophet. In this case it is not difficult to reconstruct the nature of these groups. Jeremiah is a member of one of the priestly families of Anathoth (Jer. 1:1), the city to which the High Priest Abiathar and his Ephraimite priestly relatives had been exiled by Solomon (1 Kgs. 2:26-27). This priestly line is traditionally associated with the old northern sanctuary at Shiloh and may be related to the carriers of the Deuteronomistic theological traditions. We have already noted that Jeremiah is a supporter of those traditions, and it is clear that he also accepted Deuteronomistic views on prophecy. This is particularly obvious in the account of his call, which portrays him as a "prophet like Moses," a particular type of prophet playing a prominent role in Deuteronomistic tradition (Jer. 1:4-10; cf. Deut. 18:9-22). It is therefore likely that Jeremiah's supporters were among those groups that accepted the Deuteronomistic theology and that they viewed him as a legitimate Mosaic prophet (Jeremiah 26). However, it is clear that Jeremiah was a peripheral figure who was not part of the central religious establishment in Jerusalem. His oracles seem to have had no impact on anyone but his own supporters, and his message was strongly opposed by the Jerusalemite establishment, which saw him as a madman rather than as a true prophet (Jer. 20:1-6; 29:24-28; 36:1-32).[14]

Hananiah's acceptance of the Jerusalemite royal theology and his position in the royal court suggest that he was a central prophet who was a part of Jerusalem's religious establishment. His supporters were to be found in this group, which preserved the old traditions of God's eternal election of the city. He undoubtedly viewed Jeremiah as a threat to the social order whose oracles simply undermined the people's traditional faith.

The conflict between Jeremiah and Hananiah was therefore not only a conflict between different theological positions but was also a confrontation between two prophets having different social locations and different supporters. Jeremiah, the peripheral prophet, and Hananiah, the central prophet, were each unwilling to recognize the prophetic claims of the other, and their supporters were also unlikely to be persuaded by the opposition's views. Hananiah did not fit the paradigm of the Mosaic prophet and so was not likely to be accredited by Jeremiah's group, and Jeremiah did not fit the Jerusalemite picture of what a prophet ought to be.

The only way of resolving this conflict was to attempt to discredit the opponent. This is precisely what Jeremiah did by making use of false prophecy accusations. On a number of occasions he complains that the Jerusalemite prophets have spoken visions from their own minds rather than the true word of God (Jer. 23:16-17). They have not stood in the Divine Council but have spoken ineffective words that did not come true (Jer. 23:18, 21-22). Unlike Mosaic prophets such as Jeremiah, the Jerusalemites have relied on dreams and have copied words from one another instead of speaking the direct word of God, which can always be recognized because of its effectiveness (Jer. 23:25-32; cf. Num. 12:6-8; Deut. 18:21-22).

However, Jeremiah's charges are more than simple false prophecy accusations, for in his theological tradition false prophecy was

14. For a more comprehensive account of Jeremiah's background and theological views, see Wilson, *Prophecy and Society*, pp. 231-51.

punishable by death (Deut. 18:20). Seen in this light, false prophecy accusations have the same function as witchcraft accusations do in modern societies. In the face of deteriorating social conditions, Jeremiah risked shattering the Jerusalemite social structure by attempting to remove Hananiah permanently from the scene. According to the biblical tradition, Jeremiah succeeded in his attempt. His false prophecy accusation ultimately led to Hananiah's death (Jer. 28:12–17).

VI

Sociology and the Future of Old Testament Studies

The use of social-scientific data in biblical studies is now in its infancy, and it is still too soon to predict the influence that this sort of comparative approach may have. However, even the small amount of work that has already been done allows us to make three generalizations about the course that future research should take.

THE UNFINISHED SOCIOLOGICAL AGENDA

Just as Old Testament scholars have only recently become aware of the potential usefulness of the work being done by social scientists, so social scientists are just beginning to realize that biblical scholars can contribute to social-scientific research. This mutual awareness of the fruitfulness of interdisciplinary conversation has led to important gains on both sides, but now, at least from the standpoint of biblical studies, the interchange needs to be carried one step farther. The application of social-scientific methods has led biblical scholars to explore new interpretive options and to ask new questions of their material. However, to answer some of these questions it will be necessary to have sociological data not presently available. This data can only come from new research, and biblical scholars now need to collaborate with their colleagues in the social sciences to set new agendas for sociological studies. In the area of historiography, for example, it would be useful for the historian of ancient Israel to have more information about the decay of lineage systems and about the factors that influence the development of new organizational systems. Power relationships within monarchical states also need to be studied more fully. At the same time, literary critics would be aided by having additional data on the way in which oral literature functions in specific social settings and on the changes that take place when oral literature is preserved in writing. In the end such an expansion into new areas should be mutually enriching and should break new ground in both fields.

SOCIOLOGY AND TRADITIONAL
METHODS OF INTERPRETATION

The cross-disciplinary research that has been done up to this point indicates the usefulness of using social-scientific approaches in the study of Israelite history, literature, and religion, but it is clear that the sociological approach cannot be conceived as a new method capable of replacing more traditional ones. Rather, explorations of the social dimensions of the Old Testament world are most useful when employed in conjunction with more traditional interpretive tools, such as form and tradition criticism, literary criticism, archaeology, and comparative linguistics. When used as an adjunct to more traditional approaches to the Old Testament, sociology can sometimes broaden them or make them more effective. As we have already seen, comparative sociological material can supply the form critic with a more sophisticated understanding of the social settings in which literary forms function and can give the literary critic a clearer sense of the interaction between language and society. To the archaeologist social scientists can suggest new questions to ask of ancient evidence. In this way a sociological approach can sometimes sharpen the traditional skills of the interpreter and historian.

However, the limitations of a sociological approach must always be kept in mind, and it must be recognized that not every interpretive or historical problem can be solved by applying such an approach. The most useful skill which the interpreter or historian can develop is the ability to determine which exegetical tools are most likely to yield significant results.

Although sociological approaches to the Old Testament in no way supercede more traditional methods, an awareness of the sociological dimensions of a text or a historical phenomenon does sometimes cause the interpreter to question the *results* of those methods. This is so particularly where a traditional approach has provided a narrow interpretation that ignores social context. Thus, for example, once the sociological aspects of prophecy have been recognized, it is difficult not to have doubts about interpretations of prophetic literature that treat the prophet as a completely isolated individual. However, the quarrel in this case is with the results of a traditional method or with its application, not with the method itself.

SOCIOLOGY AND
OLD TESTAMENT THEOLOGY

Finally, the use of sociological approaches has pointed to the role of social factors in shaping Old Testament religion and literature. Both the religion and the literature may be divinely inspired, but that inspiration was mediated by human agents who were thoroughly integrated into their societies and who were molded by social forces. Similar social factors influence the reading and interpretation of the Old Testament in the present day. Both of these facts need to be taken into account in future research on Old Testament theology. It is no longer possible to engage in theological reflection without taking into account the role of the Old Testament's social matrix. Both ancient Israel and the sacred text that it produced were part of a complex cultural system, and the theological implications of this fact must now be explored.